A REVOLUTIONARY LESSON PLANNING FRAMEWORK FOR TEACHING THE WHOLE LEARNER

INSPIRING JOY

JENNIFER APPEL

Inspiring. JOY: A Revolutionary Lesson Planning Framework for Teaching the Whole Learner

Published by Award Winning Culture Kennewick, WA
awardwinningculture.com

Cover Design and Illustrations by Jennifer Appel
Editing and Interior Design by Award Winning Culture

Paperback ISBN: 978-1-7350585-4-2
ebook ISBN: 978-1-7350585-5-9
First Printing: August 2021

<u>D</u>edication

To Hans, thank you for being you and making my life better
just by being in it. You are an amazing dad to our puppies and
an even better partner.

Lindsay—
You are an amazing coach
and friend to all :") Thank-you for
your constant honesty and commitment!
Thank-you for being an Award
Winning Educator! #InspiringJOY

Jennifer Appel

Table of Contents

Forward

"History will judge us by the difference we make in the everyday lives of children."
-Nelson Mandela

In the early 80's, I had the privilege of leading an elementary school in rural Washington. While supporting a building came with daily challenges, I was incredibly honored to serve my community as principal to a high energy home of our best and brightest youth. In 30+ years in education I was fortunate to work with thousands of learners--eager to make their mark on the world. While many students stood out through my years, there was always something special about one small fiery blond child named Jennifer, who seemed destined to light the educational world on fire.

I vividly remember her lining up stuffed animals to read picture books to them as she experimented with various dramatic voices and unique characters. As a young person, she thrived on being underestimated and was incessantly driven to prove she could succeed, despite early learning struggles. As she catapulted onto middle school she frequently returned to my building to help out, and soak up the school system like an instructional sponge. During volunteering visits she made copies, decorated newsletters, babysat children during parent nights, and relished any other chance to be a part of something bigger than herself.

Beyond her former principal, I was lucky enough to coach her in basketball for many years. As the standout point guard, she loved serving up the ball for others to discover success. It was no surprise that in high school she set her sights on a future in education and even worked as a paraprofessional at my school during one summer.

As veteran teachers understand, having a positive relationship with a student that spans decades can be life-changing. While Jennifer moved away to college, I stayed connected to her as she prepared for her future work as a teacher. And it won't surprise you that 4 years later, when it was time to set up and organize her first classroom, she chose to give me a call to come help. Immediately she demonstrated an expertise for the art of teaching coupled with a passion to guide her students to success.

FORWARD

Amazingly, only a couple years into her career as a high impact teacher, I found her sitting in the front row of my Masters of Literacy program at Heritage University, she was the first woman in her family to earn a Master's degree. Shortly after completing her program, this talented educator was quickly snatched up to teach college level classes. As an award winning teacher by day and adjunct professor at night, Jennifer continued to make all my wildest occupational predictions for her educational potential come true. A highlight for me, was co-teaching masters level classes with my former prized student. As a true leader, she excelled in providing future teachers with compelling feedback to help them grow. In truth, I have never seen better skills as a teacher!

At my retirement party, family, friends, and colleagues stood up to deliver heartfelt speeches about my career impact. But the most compelling moment came when Jennifer detailed the personal and professional influence in which I had on her pursuing her childhood dream.

Reflecting on this little 5 year old girl, who I watched climb onto the tall yellow school bus, with tears filling my eyes; who would've thought she'd grow up to become such a profoundly inspiring educator, speaker, and author.

Of course, looking back, I did; because I am her DAD. Her mom (Jan) and I saw that twinkle of JOY, from the moment she was born.

--Paul Dowdy, Retired Award Winning Principal, College Professor, and Program Director

Introduction

"Lessons often come dressed up as detours and roadblocks."
-Oprah Winfrey

With high stakes testing, over reliance on teacher and student compliance, and increasing political unraveling of our educational purpose, I've felt a strong pressure to detour from the culture focused classroom that resides in my heart. Teachers' own expertise have given way to canned curriculum delivered to uninspired anxiety ridden learners. Education can and SHOULD BE so much more than preparing students for the next test, grade level, or future career.

And I should know...

I was quite literally born and raised to become a teacher. Education runs through my veins like salt in the ocean. It's in my DNA! As a proud fourth generation educator, I come from a long line of impactful servant leaders.

My father was an incredible elementary teacher, principal, and college professor. My mom worked as a dedicated paraprofessional at all levels from preschool to high school before transitioning to an administrative role helping run the education department for a local university. My grandmother was a hardworking cook in the schools. My great grandfather was an engaging teacher, principal, and superintendent. My brother is a successful principal and his wife is a wonderful middle school science teacher. Even non educational family members somehow chose careers to help serve others: nurse, doctor, car mechanic, and minister.

Original telegram offering my great-grandfather his
first principalship in Washington State.

3

INTRODUCTION

I can't ever remember a time that I didn't want to be a teacher. In fact, as a child, I would transform my bedroom into a fantasy classroom to instruct my Care Bears and Snoopys how to cook, read, or create funny characters from playdough. Those lucky stuffed animals learned so many special lessons. I had a gift for storytelling and a passion for creativity while nurturing others.

Every single summer job I had, either related directly to education or working with kids. With such a laser focused vision for my future, it might be crazy for one to imagine my journey to foster this JOY has been paved with unexpected adversity.

> *"In school, you're taught a lesson and then given a test.*
> *In life, you're given a test that teaches you a lesson."*
> *-Tom Bodett*

→ Who could've guessed that the little girl afraid of the neighborhood dog, would grow up to love her own animals as a substitute for being unable to have children of her own...

→ Who could've thought that an adolescent young woman finding herself in a toxic relationship with an abusive boyfriend, might one day relish the opportunity to work with the school's most violent and aggressive teen boys...

→ Who could've believed that the child who 'couldn't read,' would transform into an award winning reading specialist fueled by a gift for prose...

→ Who could've predicted that the gritty athlete's toughest opponents would actually become two life-long incurable diseases...

→ Who could've foreshadowed an already successful teacher being willing to completely reinvent herself, classroom, and cultural philosophy...

LIFE'S LESSONS ILLUMINATE A PATH TOWARD SPECTACULAR JOY, WHEN WE IGNITE THE FLAME OF SELF-REFLECTION.

I'm eternally grateful for my husband, Hans Appel's book *Award Winning Culture* for sharing a school-wide framework to intentionally reach the whole child by remembering, "education at its highest level is about inspiring others to discover and develop their JOY."

But how do we take this idealistic vision for what schools can become and actually foster the individual classroom culture to create such a grassroots movement toward reimagining education?

> *"If there is a book you want to read but isn't written yet, write it."*
> -Shel Silverstein

In writing this sequel, I want to bravely inspire with unapologetic vulnerability to hold up a shiny metaphoric mirror for teachers to explore their own talent to touch human lives. My hope for you in reading this book is to share some of my personal and professional struggles to help us all learn and grow together. Beyond the individual wisdom from reading my story, my greatest wish is that you feel compelled and even EMPOWERED to reflect on your life lessons to help guide yourself toward reaching your own vision for inspiring JOY.

Not a temporary feeling of happiness. But real sustainable--deep in your soul--kinda JOY.

JOY is the mindful acknowledgement of humanistic alignment.

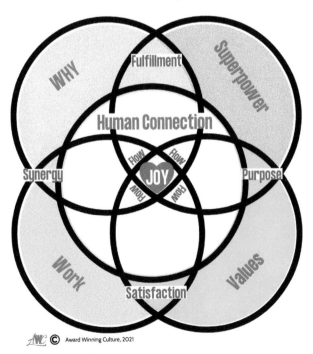

Award Winning Culture, 2021

Introduction

Teaching isn't about imparting wisdom; it's about unlocking a student's internal joy to learn. And true joy is found at the intersection of our why, superpower, work, and values, all within our human connections. Teachers who chase joy cast a net filled with purpose, fulfillment, deep satisfaction, and synergy toward remarkable human potential.

However, this heart work can feel overwhelming and unattainable in this inside the box world of education. Teachers need a way to support this life changing work, without feeling added pressure, from one more thing on their plates.

Some folks believe that they must have a special degree to teach SEL, Character, and other life skills. NO---NO---NO!

All educators are SEL teachers. The only question...is how intentional are you being with your influence?

This whole child work must be embedded into EVERYTHING we do; because they're watching, learning, and listening--even when you don't realize you're teaching.

Marrying academic content with instructing the whole learner is the holy grail of teaching. Thus, the gold standard for lesson planning is a system for infusing the two together...

This can and MUST become part of our lessons we are already teaching. If you are teaching math, english, physical education, art, science, etc. it doesn't matter--all of these skills can be taught within your curriculum.

Throughout this book you'll discover my solution: LESSICONS. LESSICONS is a template for achieving pedagogical joy.

 LAUNCH (Inspiring JOY and Purpose)

The intention of the LAUNCH is to inspire joy and purpose to start the lesson. This can be accomplished in many different ways, telling a story, asking questions, reviewing concepts, entry tasks, or daily check-in. Inspired learning is about making connections with your students rather than requiring them to regurgitate information. The key to remember with a launch is to FIRE UP the learner to take flight.

 EXPECTATIONS (Healthy, Challenged, Supported, Engaged and Safe)

EXPECTATIONS go beyond the standards you are 'expected' to teach. How will you challenge the students? How will you ensure they feel supported? What ways will you intentionally engage the learners? Lastly, how might your standards leave students feeling safe and healthy? [Example: suppose one of your expectations is to use socratic seminars to foster critical thinking among your students. While this is a great technique to use, teachers must pre-plan ways to help students feel comfortable with civil discourse. Creating this environment may require pre-teaching, modeling, and practicing how to have an effective discussion and how to disagree respectfully. Skipping this cultural work can impact the harmony, collaboration, and trust that leads to meaningful learning.]

▭▭▷ STUFF (Culturally Responsive Materials)

The STUFF in a lesson refers to all of the culturally responsive materials you will need for your project. [Examples: A project that requires markers to complete the assignment will be supported with teachers having "TO GO" markers available for students because some learners don't have markers available in their home. Outdated text filled with biased language, references, and imagery MUST be given a proper facelift to provide relevant content that each and every student can enjoy.]

 SKILLS

These social emotional learning SKILLS address five broad and interrelated areas: **self-awareness, self-management, social awareness, relationship skills, and responsible decision-making** (CASEL.org). Circle which element(s) will be in your lesson to help stay focused on reinforcing these critical soft skills into each class period--while some lessons may have just one element, others might address all 5. Example: classroom group work provides an opportunity to develop student relationship skills. According to CASEL.org relationship skills include:

- Communicating effectively
- Developing positive relationships
- Demonstrating cultural competency
- Resolving conflicts constructively
- Practicing teamwork and collaborative problem-solving
- Resisting negative social pressure
- Showing leadership in groups
- Standing up for the rights of others
- Seeking or offering support and help when needed

INSTRUCTION/ACTIVITIES (Focus on Relationships)

INSTRUCTION and/or activities must include opportunities to incorporate relationship building and inclusion. This could include the format for delivery of instruction. [I.E teachers might focus on student centered strategies that foster voice, choice and agency--rather than a traditional lecture style format. Additionally, inclusion should be paramount to lesson designing. How will I engage introverted learners, students of color, or a variety of learning styles?] Whatever format my instruction takes should be highly supportive of fostering relationships (peer-to-peer and student-teacher).

CLOSE INTENTIONALLY (Character, Excellence, and Community)

Teachers who are driven to inspire joy recognize that every instructional ending provides an opportunity to CLOSE INTENTIONALLY. The closure of your lesson, can not be: put your books away or here's the homework assignment. Teachers must focus on Character, Excellence, and Community as a catalyst to impact the learning culture beyond the classroom. Having the students thinking about how they will do the right thing, did they do their very best, or what they will do for others.

OPPORTUNITIES (Personalized, Equitable, Enriched, Targeted, and Intensive Support)

Teachers who dial up OPPORTUNITIES, within their lessons incorporate personalization to all students. These extensions might take many forms: whole class, small group or individuals--but uniquely allow learners enrichment, and/or targeted intensive support. Equity is a key element of providing opportunity to ALL LEARNERS. Removing barriers leads to engagement and productivity, while promoting inclusivity. Teachers can ask: is this lesson accessible, relevant, and worthwhile to EACH student?

NEEDS (Formative and Summative Assessment through a trauma informed lens)

NEEDS, might be better known as assessment. Informal assessments include surveys, polls, check-ins, or observations as teachers determine their students readiness for learning. Viewing needs through a trauma informed lens keeps educators planning for a culture of safety that truly meets students where they are. Teachers who create needs based assessments, directly communicate to their students that they are valued, important and capable of learning. [I.E: Rather than viewing traditional assessments through a content focused lens--educators view learning on a continuum within a humanistic lens. No longer is memorization, regurgitation, and answering potentially person biased questions overvalued.] Teachers who focus on needs, ensure that the learning data they acquire is filled with rich context populated with real student faces.

SELF-REFLECTION (Social Emotional Learning reflection for students and teacher)

SELF-REFLECTION goes far beyond analyzing a student's success on a concept because award winning teachers recognize that learning goes far beyond academic content. Reflecting on social emotional learning aspects of the lesson helps the teacher and student evaluate life's progress. Are students working well in groups? Do they feel confident in their abilities to connect and work interpersonally with others? Did I account for inequities in the lessons? Self-reflection might be a soft skill targeted exit ticket, check-out, or mindful moment [I.E: when teachers reflect on learning addition in math that day, they can boldly ask: How are you feeling about learning addition? Is there anything I can do as your teacher to help you? Did you have any conflicts during group work today?] Self-Reflection strengthens metacognitive skills amongst everyone in the learning process.

A teacher who's lesson plan focuses only on academics is like a coach who only teaches her players to dunk a basketball. They might be missing key skills like dazzling dribbling, pinpoint passing, sharp shooting, or gritty rebounding. Let's not forget endurance, sportsmanship, or leadership. It also assumes that everyone is capable of dunking without modifications like a smaller ball, lower rim, or trampoline to jump higher. Perhaps, they're not even showing up to the gym with proper equipment like an adequate pair of shoes or deflated ball. How good would our team actually be if everyone only knew how to dunk? Furthermore, some athletes don't even want to play basketball at all--they'd opt out in favor of volleyball, football, or tennis.

LESSICONS help teachers focus on the entire team of whole learners.

Beyond heartfelt messaging, this book will provide you with practical strategies while providing places to jot notes and questions to push your thinking. It's formatted exactly like a lesson plan book, with 3 units, Character, Excellence, and Community. Within those units each chapter is set up using the LESSICONS format with practical ideas. At the end of each unit, I include a sample universal lesson plan adaptable to any age.

"Life must be understood backward. But it must be lived forward."
-Soren Kierkegaard

Everything in life...happens for a reason. This book has landed in your hands for a reason--I'm thrilled for you to joyfully go forward and reexamine your own classroom!

Share out your reflections using #InspiringJOY

UNIT 1: CHARACTER

Let's reflect back to *Award Winning Culture*. In his book, Appel breaks down a multi-step framework to intentionally infuse social emotional learning and character development into the daily fabric of the school. From selecting a whole child curriculum all the way to best practice implementation strategies, Appel walks readers through: articulating vision, gathering buy-in, creating a T.E.A.M, and a complete rollout to impact culture and climate. Beyond a school-wide model to reach cultural success, readers examine a host of strategies and examples that help elevate kindness, empathy, and service across all areas of learning. Indeed, no school-wide stone is left unturned during Appel's dissection of ways to keep character education front and center with activities, experiential learning, and rewards. But perhaps, his thorough examination of ongoing training, accountability, and creating a common language are what elevates this section to rarified ere in school culture work. Appel then finishes with specific ideas to highlight and remind all stakeholders of the power of doing the right thing.

BUT HOW MIGHT THIS SCHOOL CULTURE MASTERPIECE ACTUALLY PLAY OUT IN THE CLASSROOM SETTING?

During Unit 1, I'll be expanding on all 9 elements of CHARACTER and providing teachers with a blueprint for applying this critical work to our own classrooms. Character should no longer be a stand alone item. Through intentionality and action, educators have the ability to teach, model, and reinforce how to create joyful spaces for all learners to practice character.

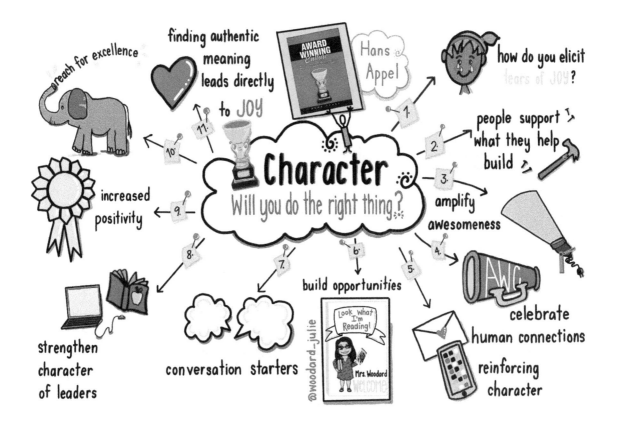

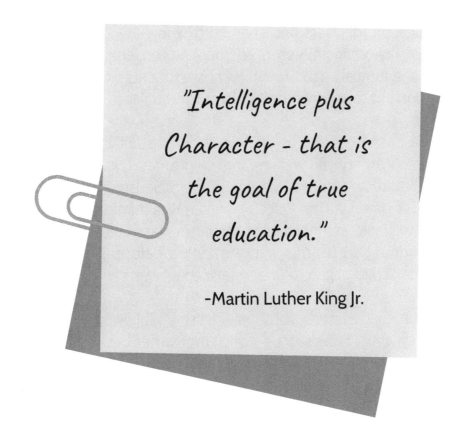

"Intelligence plus Character - that is the goal of true education."

-Martin Luther King Jr.

LESSON 1:

JURENKA-CURRICULUM

 **Launch:**

"What's the most popular book for 5th grade boys," she asked?

I heard a few other people answer incorrectly before I finally got up the nerve to say, "Guiness Book of World Records". And I was right, I remember her giving me a look, like...WHO ARE YOU? Clearly, the question was meant to stump everyone in the room and when it didn't...I had immediately captured Jurenka's attention.

Dr. Jurenka was the first and most memorable college professor in the reading department, at Central Washington University. As a cute older woman in her early 60's, she had been in education for years and seemed to know EVERYTHING about kids and READING. She was not like other professors I'd encountered; she didn't start out with the syllabus, or lecture-- she jumped right in. While most students were intimidated by her, I managed to have an instant connection based on our mutual love of reading.

One day, I arrived into class while she began to present. Instantly, she looked over at me, and STOPPED and said, "Why are you wearing that shirt today?" Making my way toward the nearest open seat, I told her it was March 2nd--Dr. Seuss's birthday and this was considered Read Across America Day. Once again she was a little taken back by me, and not really sure what to think, as no other students in class were aware of this special Seuss remembrance (don't forget—this was the 1990's before it was a hugely famous day). Immediately, Jurenka had begun to understand that I was serious about education.

Soon after, we were assigned our first vocabulary lesson. I followed the directions exactly as was stated on the syllabus. I was such a compliant learner back then. I was convinced that I'd dazzle my beloved professor. Several days later, my world was turned upside down as I got the assignment back and received a C on the assignment. I know a C doesn't sound like the end of the world...but to me...in that moment...as Jurenka's prized student...it felt like a big fat FAILURE!

Now, I didn't get C's...EVER...maybe a B in Econ 301 sophomore year, but that was it. I was an A student and particularly devastated because this was a class that I thought I was excelling in and taught by a teacher who really liked me. Naturally, I connected with Jurenka after class to ask what I could do to improve. Truth be told, I wanted an explanation of what part of the assignment I didn't complete.

After telling me I had followed the directions exactly from the syllabus, I began to feel more confused and frustrated than ever. Why wouldn't she have given me an A? Jurenka went on:

"No you don't understand, you didn't have any passion or personality in your lesson, it was just the facts, you were following a formula. That is not what teaching is about, you can do much better than this. I expect so much more from YOU."

Initially, I was pissed off and thought she doesn't know what she is talking about. Other students in class had received higher grades with lower quality work. Why would she grade students differently based on the same rubric? I did exactly what I was told to do! Why was she picking on me? Am I not cut out to be a reading teacher? The negative self-talk furiously revolved through my head like a disaster rolodex.

Emotions tell us a story about the things we care about.

Have you ever wondered why the student who pushes all your buttons in class is the one who keeps you up at night? Teachers are DESPERATE to reach our most challenging learners. Our emotions with our at-risk kiddos provide a pathway to how we view good teaching.

Pride leads to overconfidence and hypocriticalness while humility allows us to rethink our actions.

I slowly started thinking about my Jurenka story from another perspective. Was she right? Did I fail to pour my heart and soul into the assignment? Was I simply going through the motions? In this soul searching weekend of reflection, I realized that she was challenging me in a meaningful way! I didn't interject any of MY personality into my lesson and I certainly didn't add any excitement or fun for the students. I treated it like it was an assignment rather than my life's passion. I was focused on following the directions, not creating a lesson that inspired curiosity, engagement, and empowerment.

13

Fueled by a renewed energy to prove something to my favorite professor, I recreated the entire lesson and added my own personal touches to it. In this Creativity Peak, I added a few read-alouds for the students to teach the vocabulary. When I was done with my masterpiece, it was an amazing lesson and I was thrilled to show it to my professor. She was beyond pleased with my fervor for teaching in the new lesson plan and gave me an A.

"I KNEW you could do better Jennifer," Jurenka validated.

While the A felt satisfying, in that moment, I realized it wasn't about the A at all, it was about me growing, learning, and striving to get the approval of Jurenka. Somehow she saw something inside of me that was special and in order to wake that part of me up, she elected to disrupt my learning with that uncomfortable first letter grade.

> TEACHERS WHO INSPIRE JOY INTENTIONALLY MEET STUDENTS WHERE THEY ARE AND INDIVIDUALLY CHALLENGE THEM TO RAISE THEIR GAME.

That moment stuck with me throughout my next two years in the program as Jurenka became my advisor; ultimately, helping me flourish through my educational preparation. I am eternally grateful for Dr. Jurenka and what she taught me about reading; but moreover, what she taught me about exceptional teaching. It's imperative to have fun and let your personality shine through. I'll never forget that takeaway and I think about her often when a lesson doesn't work out the way I intended.

> IN THE END...WE MUST CHECK OUR EGO AT THE DOOR IN ORDER TO BE AN OUTSTANDING EDUCATOR! HUMILITY PROVIDES OTHERS THE OPPORTUNITY TO HELP YOU UNCOVER THE GREAT EDUCATOR...YOU'RE MEANT TO BE!

Reimagining your curriculum!

 Expectations: Educators must infuse themselves into their curriculum.

 Stuff: YOU!!!

 Skills: Self-Awareness, think about your own strengths, why, values, personality, and passions.

 ## Instruction/Activities:

How many times have you had a new idea or initiative introduced at your school or district? As an educator for over 20 years, I have seen this happen A LOT! Teachers generally have two reactions to this: ignore it and hope it all goes away, or go all in and basically throw out everything else they've done to this point.

When given a new curriculum, we have to incorporate it in with our why. As teachers, we all have a very distinct mix of personality, experience, and training. Educators can't lose themselves by simply reading from a canned curriculum.

For instance, the first SEL curriculum I taught years ago was super dry, outdated, and stale. The videos depicted students who looked straight out of the 1980's. It reminded me of those cheesy human growth type videos that make you feel like you're in a really bad after school special movie. Needless to say, some teachers threw everything out and didn't teach it. Still, other educators stuck to the script and delivered painful doses of social emotional well-being from this tired program.

But, I knew that the information in this curriculum was really important, even if the packaging needed a serious update. Determined to find a way to support my students, I looked at the curriculum and pulled out the main ideas from each unit, gathered the materials that were appropriate for my students, and then created modified lessons that fit my why, my personality and my classroom.

For instance, during one conflict resolution lesson, I wrote out multiple scripts for kids to dive into the work firsthand. A group of my boys acted out a dispute during a pick up basketball game at lunch. Resolving lunchtime conflict was such a relevant endeavor, I knew it'd resonate with my students. Students acted out fouling each other and then yelling about how the foul wasn't fair, etc.. They had lots of fun pretending and overacting for the lesson. The scene was complete with jerseys, nerf basketball, and mini hoop. After each group, we then had a class discussion breaking apart all of the elements of this incident to see how we could resolve the conflict and how bystanders could help or hinder in this situation.

My students had to be challenged during this exercise. Sometimes you have to put the ownership back on the students. Who is causing this situation and why are the bystanders just as guilty? This kind of activity lets me push the limits with my students and challenge them in the same ways that Jurenka did for me. Abandoning the cheesy prompts allowed my students to wrestle with the critical messages.

REFLECTION REALLY HELPS DRIVE DEEPER LEARNING HOME.

We had a passionate discussion uncovering feelings, action, and thoughts and were able to come up with some ideas on how to resolve a similar conflict in the future. While the lesson started with common language and big ideas from the actual curriculum, what really elevated this to a memorable experience was the individualized skit and guided reflection.

 ## Close Intentionally:

TEACHERS--have confidence in yourself and understand that YOU have the right and more importantly the RESPONSIBILITY to customize curriculum to make it work for your students, content, and environment. My challenge for you is to look at your curriculum with a critical eye. What key concepts do the students need to learn and then add personalization to the lesson for your specific learners.

 ## Opportunities:

Anytime you have a curriculum (SEL, character, or academic content) you will always have the choice to personalize or modify the assignment, to make it truly award winning. This concept was made very clear to me in the first 3 years of teaching our CharacterStrong curriculum (Norlin/Kraft). The curriculum is amazing and has excellent practical applications which the students love. In fact, my students yearly "standardized reading scores went up almost 2 years of growth" after infusing these whole learner principles into my language arts class (Appel, 2018).

That being said, I was teaching the same advisory class for 3 years. Thus, I would have the same group of students as 6th, 7th, and 8th graders. This was a challenge given the fact that I was primarily a 6th grade teacher. Personalization showed up in my matching instructional choice to student grade level. No longer did I need to rewrite the curriculum; however, I was absolutely intentional with my delivery based on their age and maturity level. Thus, our discussions and reflections were targeted based on meeting them where they're at.

> TEACHERS CAN TRULY REACH THEIR STUDENTS WHEN THEY PERSONALIZE THEIR CURRICULUM DELIVERY BASED ON THE CURRENT LEARNERS.

 ## Needs:

Creating a personalized pre-assessment is a great way to find out what your students already know and what direction you need to take the curriculum. Personalized pre-assessment include not only concepts, but questions about strengths, growth areas, and how students feel about certain subjects. Canned curriculums are based on a predetermined set of standards and the pre-assessments that accompany them are based solely on concepts. By doing personalized pre-assessments you are able to assess concepts, but also strengths, growth areas, and feelings. With this knowledge you are then able to tailor the lessons for your class, by helping students make personal connections beyond the scope of the curriculum.

 ## Self-Reflection:

How can we better infuse our passion, personality, and purpose while ensuring a culturally responsive curriculum?

Are YOU willing to acknowledge when you're operating at C quality work?

Who gives you authentic feedback on your teaching?

What is a moment from your life, that pushes you to stay true to your own why?

How might you intentionally challenge specific students to dig deeper to magnify the light inside of them?

Share out your reflections using #InspiringJOY

AFFIRMATIONS

(Write, Draw, or Brainstorm ideas or thoughts here)

I AM A CURRICULUM LEADER BECAUSE...

Jennifer Appel inspires readers to reflect on personal life lessons to help us navigate toward creating and reaching our vision, inspiring joy in others. Picking up this book is an ESSENTIAL step in the right direction if you seek fulfillment within teaching and are looking to support learners in their journey to find happiness through meaningful learning experiences. *Inspiring Joy* provides **PRACTICAL STRATEGIES** to help move our ideas to action, creating the best opportunities for the whole child!

**Elisabeth Bostwick, Educator, Speaker, and
Author of Take the L.E.A.P.: Ignite a Culture of Innovation**

LESSON 2:

BE YOU! - HIGHLIGHTS

 Launch:

When I was in college, my dream was to become a 2nd grade teacher. I got a degree in elementary education with a K-12 reading endorsement. My practicums, student teaching, and internships were all in 2nd grade. After graduating, I was thrilled to learn of a 2nd grade job opening up and I thought it'd be perfect for me. I was so excited by the mere opportunity to potentially work in my desired position.

Completely pumped for my interview, I had a portfolio of my work including a scrapbook of pictures from all of my different experiences. I was ready and completely confident for this interview. After the interview, I felt pretty good. I could answer all of the questions and loved that they were clearly engaged with what I was saying.

A few days later I finally received a highly anticipated call from the principal in which she informed me that I would NOT be getting the job. I was so bummed!

My husband was a career counselor at the time, and had always told me if you ever don't get a job it's a good idea to ask why so you can discover if there was something that could be improved upon for the next interview. While I was upset and slightly embarrassed, I took the plunge and dug deeper. WHY NOT ME??

She said very nicely, ***"well, you had just a little too much energy for us. You were just a little too positive and energetic--I don't think you would fit in with our school."***

Feeling shocked and hurt, I managed a brief *"thank you"* and hung up the phone. Disappointment often fuels human connection. My dad immediately received a call from me. I told him what she said and my dad kindly told me that it probably worked out for the best. He reinforced to me that if they didn't want someone that was positive and energetic in an elementary school, maybe that wasn't where I was supposed to work.

Reflecting on dad's words, I made my way home eager to chat with Hans all about it.

I explained to him that my plan for the next interview was to tone it down and try not to be so positive. In my head, I had gotten the message loud and clear—BE MORE SERIOUS. I was determined to be less excited about wanting to be a teacher and not nearly as positive about my life's passion. As if I could just take the essence of myself, remove it, and set it on a shelf.

My brilliant husband told me I was crazy, and that I should "NEVER change who you are for a job." He reminded me that I was special because of my positive energy and not to let anyone force me to change into something that I wasn't. After all, my unique passion and love for education, kids, and reading WAS my superpower! NOT magnifying the best parts of me would be a recipe for failure and unhappiness.

Ironically, I was offered three different jobs in the next week, with all administrators citing it was because I had such a positive energetic vibe and they were convinced I could bring something great to their school.

We have to be who we are...

> **Teachers practicing authenticity in the classroom not only live a more joyful existence...they inspire joy in their learners.**

We have to surround ourselves with people who remind us to use our superpowers--not hide them. We can't let others bring us down to their level or try to make us something we don't believe in. We are all unique and can be empathetic without compromising who we are.

> **Teachers who inspire JOY stay true to themselves and encourage students to do the same.**

Students should feel compelled to be themselves in your room when you show respect and admiration for their authentic selves.

 Expectations: Highlighting students' unique talents helps them to develop success in and out of the classroom.

Stuff: Teachers will respect students and their unique traits, diversity, and background while relating to them as a whole person, and reinforce how they can use those gifts to become fulfilled.

 Skills: You are modeling social and self awareness by respecting that each student is unique. And having students demonstrate relationship skills by getting to know their classmates on a more personal level.

Instruction/Activities:

Establishing student relationships from the beginning of the year gives you the advantage of getting to know them on a personal level to truly uncover who they are and how they learn.

One cool idea is to create a featured STAR student of the week. By regularly highlighting a student in your class, they're able to bring in pictures, a poster, or personal items to share with the class.

> THIS FORM OF PERSONAL STORYTELLING ALLOWS TEACHERS AND FELLOW CLASSMATES TO CONNECT IN MEANINGFUL WAYS.

I mean who didn't love show and tell in Kindergarten. It is a great way to get to know your students and understand their strengths.

Why would we ever stop doing this after kindergarten?

Providing a regular platform for a 7th grade teen or a high school senior to showcase their passion, culture and identity can be just as powerful, when we use a bit of intentionality. Highlighting student's strengths gives them the insight to harness their skills to use them to their advantage. And uncovering student skills and passions provides us a path toward connecting them to our academic content while fostering character rich environments.

One year, I had a leadership student who everyone had told me was super quiet (I MEAN LIKE PAINFULLY SHY) and probably shouldn't have even been in the class, as she seemed to be afraid of her own shadow. Mistakenly believing that leadership was for extroverts only, my colleagues thought her placement was just a bad idea for everyone. However, as

22

we learned from Susan Cain, in her book, *Quiet*, introverts can be tremendous leaders and bring a host of overlooked talents. Outgoingness is such a huge misconception. I was determined to find what this student was exceptional at and then highlight her passion as a means of magnifying the depths of her social influence.

As it turned out, she had what business leadership guru Jack Welch might call the "generosity gene" which unlike outgoingness is absolutely correlated with leadership aptitude. Furthermore, she was one of the most artistically gifted students I've had in my entire career. I was determined to highlight her gift. For instance, in preparation for our Donuts with Dudes event, she determined that we needed tiny paper cut out donuts with the words 'thank you', to give away. Naturally, she made these amazingly cute paper donuts—they looked exactly like real donuts! It was crazy how passionate she could get when tapping into her creativity.

Capitalizing on student strengths allows them to build confidence in taking other classroom risks. She led a group of students in creating these donuts, with handcrafted patterns and taught her team how to cut, fold, and assemble these eye popping giveaways. She was a born leader and it was inspiring to see her find herself by being her WHOLE self. She had a talent and when we highlighted that gift and gave her the opportunity to shine, she ran with it.

I challenge you to highlight students' talents...

One way to uncover talent is by becoming curious about a student's passions, identity, or cultural diversity. Having students take a personality test is a fun way to start a conversation. I give my students a personality test that reveals certain traits based on their answers. But the most powerful takeaways occur in reflection moments after completing these inventories. The best part is that they have such strong feelings when they feel the test is wrong. It really helps you to quickly see how they think and feel about different ideas!

Another talent revealer is to give them a quick multiple intelligences quiz to see what type of learner they are. I love to see who has what intelligence and the best part of all of these tests is the rich debate and discussion afterwards. Additionally, planning group activities becomes so much more intentional when we have non content data points on our learners.

LEARNING ABOUT EACH OTHER'S PERSONALITY, MULTIPLE INTELLIGENCES, UNIQUE CULTURAL IDENTITY, OR TALENTS CAN CREATE TRANSFORMATIVE CONNECTIONS AMONGST CLASSMATES.

Reflection is a huge part of this process; thus, students help decide if the experience was accurate and why or why not? These reflections often provide me even more insight than the actual test. My favorite part is to meet one on one with students and discuss the results and dive into what the results revealed. Students learn so much about themselves and what traits they didn't even realize were within them. I love talking about the falsities of the tests, that is where the true reflection happens. The students are usually appalled that the test results would say that and then we talk about the smaller elements within those traits and they start to really see who they are and what they truly believe. And personal introspective clarity leads directly to actionable behavior in the classroom...

 ## Close Intentionally:

Take a moment and think about the students in your room that you don't know very well. Who can you focus on this week? I'd suggest to you that if you can't pinpoint each student's superpower in one or two words--you haven't done the necessary pre-work to inspire joy.

Be relentless in your pursuit. Spend time with them and see if they will journal with you, share something with you, or communicate their passions with you.

> FIND OUT HOW TO HIGHLIGHT THEIR STRENGTHS AND MAKE IT SOMETHING THAT CAN HELP THEM THRIVE. EVERY LEARNER HAS A SUPERPOWER...WILL YOU BE THE TEACHER TO HELP THEM DISCOVER AND DEVELOP THEIR JOY?

Opportunities:

When you have students with disabilities in your classroom, are you punishing them for those things or are you using them to their advantage?

I have had many students with ADHD that struggled to sit still for a whole hour, but one particular student stands out to me. It was complete torture for him to sit for an hour! Life is on a spectrum and labels are meant to be prisms of perspective, rather than a truth for all time. Thus, I changed the structure up for him. He was able to sit in a wobble stool for the class, so that he could move around. He was given freedom to walk around the room while he read something aloud to the class. He was my helper for things that required standing up and moving. Anytime I needed a note run to the office, or to another teacher, he was my go to 'student helper.' If I needed papers handed out or needed to grab something from another spot in the room he was not only willing and able but was driven to be supportive.

These tasks weren't just an energy release or a way to distract him from misbehaving. Research actually suggests that students with ADHD think BETTER on the MOVE. By tapping into the essence of their superpower, teachers are actually waking up deeper depths of learning.

Being able to get up and move about allowed him to focus and work for the entire hour. Highlighting his disability as a strength also became a huge support system for the entire class. But allowing him to reflect on the acceptable and encouraged movement in my classroom it also helped him crystallize his beliefs in how he learned best. Furthermore, he internally shifted his self perception of 'hyperactive bad kid' to STUDENT LEADER.

> **Transforming student self perception is a game-changer to student success.**

In order to create a classroom that focuses on equity, we have to consider all learners as humans first. Emotional damage is done when students can't truly be themselves. Dena Simmons reminds educators of how "imposter syndrome" can be reinforced for students of color if we don't "center instruction on the lives, history, and identity of our students." Research tells us that students of color are suspended and expelled 3 times more often than white students. Celebrating student individualism rather than penalizing or policing it is a strong way to support "decolonizing learning" for all students (Simmons).

 **Needs:**

When you have students that are comfortable in your classroom and really shine, they are showing their true personality in your presence.

Encouraging others to maximize their trueness gives you the opportunity to highlight their strengths.

When you view student personality, passion and purpose as a class asset rather than a distraction to your teaching...you'll know that you're on your way to highlighting a student's superpower.

 Self-Reflection:

Are you criticizing students for their uniqueness or are you celebrating it?

What is a life memory that tested your belief in yourself? How do you now use it as a strength?

How might your classroom culture change when learners reframe individual student differences into recognizing peer superpowers? (Artistic, Thoughtful, Open-minded, Passionate, Skillful, Leader, etc.)

Share out your reflections using #InspiringJOY

AFFIRMATIONS

(Write, Draw, or Brainstorm ideas or thoughts here)

I am a superhero when...

Through her personal stories, Jennifer Appel compels readers to inspire joy in schools by creating powerful relationships with kids. The unique "LESSICONS" framework equips educators with a meaningful approach to educating the whole child, in a time where we need that more than ever. **THIS BOOK WILL LIFT YOU UP** and inspire you to do better in the classroom and in life!

Dr. Jacie Maslyk, Educator, Author, and Consultant

LESSON 3:
BASKETBALL FOR LIFE - ACTIVITIES

 ### Launch:

As I drove home from practice that night, I felt excruciating pain in my legs. Basketball tryouts always provided soreness as we caloused our bodies, but somehow this felt completely different. By the time I pulled into my driveway, I could literally not even move. Both knees had a constant shooting pain that I'd never felt before. My poor father had to walk out to the car and actually carry his teenage daughter into the house.

Visiting the doctor, the next day, I'd learn that I had birth defects in both knees that had finally reared their ugly heads. Apparently, all the running, jumping, and twisting was only exacerbating the problem. I left that appointment discouraged, disheartened, and down.

I was an athlete!

As the 5'4" inch starting point guard, I'd grown up preparing to be a tough, quick, rough and tumble tomboy with my eye on basketball beyond high school. As a child, I had serious boy envy. I wanted to be just like one of the guys and I did everything that my older brother Jason did--including basketball! Sports were always a huge part of our family. Our parents encouraged us to learn the team and leadership skills fostered in athletics. And I was good! Damn good! I had a great handle and played tenacious defense. Socially, my identity was so wrapped up in my athleticism.

Who am I if I can't play sports anymore?

After pushing through the pain for a while, things were getting progressively worse. My knee caps would lock so that my leg was straight and at times I couldn't even bend them. Doctors were warning me that if I continued, I might not be able to walk well when I was 40 years old. It was decision time...was it worth it to keep playing?

Following a soul searching weekend, I made the very difficult decision to quit playing sports. Walking away from an activity I loved meant a severe disruption to my self-care, routine, and identity. But moreover, it created a void in how I served my school.

Indeed, my connection to being a Hanford High School Falcon was somehow lost with the move to step away. This identity crisis damaged my confidence and led me into a dark chapter; and needless to say, life was hard for a while.

A year later, the athletic director reached out to me to become his assistant. I think he knew I longed for a way to practice and strengthen the school-wide character, I'd become known for. As the AD for a 6-12 combo middle and high school, he was pretty overwhelmed running all events and keeping the whole thing a float.

The district finally approved for him to hire an assistant. So as a 17 year old senior, I jumped back in the world of athletics. He agreed to put me in charge of the middle school, so this meant making sure the locker rooms were open for the teams. I was also responsible for running the game clocks, hiring refs, leading our bookkeeper, etc. It was a tremendous responsibility for a 17 year old, but I loved it! I was in charge of all of the sports for the entire year in middle school; thus, I was able to still feel like I was part of a team and helping others through the lens of sports leadership. This really helped me to understand that you can use your talents and passions in many different ways. I'm forever grateful to him for finding a character activity that helped me rediscover my purpose at school.

How are we involving our students in class with character defining activities? What lifelines might you throw one of your lost students?

> ## Teachers who inspire JOY create activities that support student's character development.

Finding ways to fuel your passion in untraditional avenues.

 Expectations: Educators need to involve students in the selection of activities and fuel students' passions.

 Stuff: Activities through the lens of students.

Skills: Students will practice self-management by taking ownership of their own work. They will also learn responsible decision making during the process of working with others and determining how they want to evaluate their growth.

Instruction/Activities:

Learners are capable of way more than we give them credit for. The key is to empower students to make those decisions and give them the ability to succeed or to fail...and then actively reflect on the why behind the success or failure. They have to be in charge of activities and come up with the ideas in order to feel compelled to do more.

PEOPLE TEND TO SUPPORT WHAT THEY HELP BUILD.

When you are choosing activities for your classroom. Think about these 3 things.

Evaluation

- **Student Choice** - Do you let students in your classroom vote on activities, or give input into what should be done within a unit? Do you empower your students to choose their projects for a unit of study? Students have to be given choice within the content. You might be surprised how creative students can be when it comes to expressing their knowledge. To do this, brainstorm a list of activities or projects they would like to see. Then vote from there, students will feel empowered because they were part of the planning process. Additionally, you might have pockets of the class working on different activities. Eventually, as the year goes on we have a lot more free choice for students after intentionally teaching what is expected.
- **Character** - Does the activity align with the values of your school? When you are doing anything within your classroom you always have to keep in mind what the values are within your classroom and make sure that students are going to be learning those skills in the activity.

"Values are qualities of action."
-Dr. Susan David

This is not just about academics. When you are doing an activity in your room you should always incorporate SEL into the fabric of the unit. Having a list of character traits and social emotional learning skills posted for a quick review can help you and your students build the most dynamic activities that move beyond academic content.

- **Evaluation** - This needs to be student driven. The first time I let students choose the grading practices of an activity it was uncomfortably scary for me. Cognitive Entrenchment for veteran teachers is a real issue as the longer we work in education the less likely we are to question our own assumptions. I figured they would tell me that it should be graded based on likeness, but nothing academic. As always, our students will pleasantly surprise us, when given the chance to shine. If you do the leg work at the beginning of the year and really teach Character, Excellence and Community and all of the tenets that go with it, you will empower students to make amazing choices. In the beginning there is usually a lot of debating and some students find it best to get rid of grades while others want strict grading guidelines. The solution to finding some common ground comes when we create a collaborative rubric. The students walk around the room and grade each other's projects while giving genuine feedback. Students then average the scores of the students who grade the project and their own self score. Students are able to come up with the grades and the criteria; therefore, they're completely responsible for their own learning and even what is expected.

 ## Close Intentionally:

When I quit basketball I couldn't think of another way to be involved in sports until an opportunity came my way. I might have stayed lost, if an educator hadn't directly reached out to me. Don't just have students waiting for you to create a cool activity that they might be passionate about and want to participate in. When you support them creating the activities, you are assured that they are passionate about their work and will put in every ounce of effort to accomplish that goal.

 ## Opportunities:

Differentiation is present in the teacher's mindset. Don't think about all of the ways that students CAN'T do something--think about all of the ways that they CAN! Students are way more capable of creating incredible activities than we generally give them credit for. Give them the power to make decisions and the trust to follow through.

Believing that all the best activities will come from the teacher's mind is limited thinking at best and discriminating at worse. Give your students a seat at the table of lesson design.

 ## Needs:

I knew that this experiment of giving students choice in activities was successful when I had 100% completion of the work. Every single student in my class completed the activity and they enjoyed doing it. Additionally, they were able to give each other thoughtful feedback. When they did their own evaluation they were able to see their project through a different lens and really think critically about what they could improve upon next time. Clearly, metacognition is a wonderful output of advanced student activity.

 ## Self-Reflection:

Who decides all of the lessons in your classroom? Who creates and completes the evaluations of each lesson? Why?

How can you empower students to decide on activities to further crystalize learning?

What's one life activity which has fostered the trajectory of your own passion?

Share out your reflections using **#InspiringJ🍎Y**

AFFIRMATIONS

(Write, Draw, or Brainstorm ideas or thoughts here)

I empower learners to...

Powerfully practical and precise, Jennifer Appel's passion for inspiring joy through intentionally building character, excellence, and community is infused throughout this motivating and compelling book. Every impactful, **HEART TOUCHING** story sets the stage for sample lessons as part of the fabulous framework for rich relationship and culture building opportunities. This **OUTSTANDING MUST READ** book clearly demonstrates HOW to build an award winning culture in your classroom and is an extraordinary complement to *Award Winning Culture*.

Livia Chan, Head Teacher, Author, and
Digital Content Editor for the Teach Better Team

Lesson 4:
Cool Shoes-Rewards/reinforcers

 **Launch:**

"Cool Shoes Jill," I said as I welcomed the small unassuming 6th grade girl with ash brown hair into my class one morning.

As she wandered into class, I greeted her like any other day. The entire interaction took literally LESS THAN 10 SECONDS. But as I now know, this 10 seconds meant the world to this young lady. Over the next couple months, she proudly paraded her shoes all over the school, as I was completely unaware of the impact I'd made on her.

To be honest, I forgot all about this little interaction for the remainder of the school year. Near the end of the year, I received a handwritten heartfelt letter from her mom detailing the positive impact my brief little throw-away comment made on her life.

Unbenounced to me, the "cool shoes" had been picked out by her parents. They were bright and different from her usual accessories and being a middle schooler, she found herself quite nervous about what others might think. Apparently, she had shown up to school after arguing with mom about how others might judge or tease her. My simple compliment was the kindness she needed that day.

For many middle schoolers, there's a dichotomous internal tug-a-war between hoping to be seen and desperately trying to blend in that ensures a roller coaster of emotions. My simple off hand comment to Jill, seemed to touch upon the best of both worlds.

As you can imagine, there were tears of joy as this story was shared in this heartwarming letter. If a 10 second positive compliment reinforcer can inspire a student's internal confidence and commitment to working hard, perhaps I was just beginning to understand the teacher's daily impact on a student's life success.

Teachers who inspire JOY relish all opportunities to support student motivation, confidence, and self-discovery.

My brief encounter over a pair of 'shoes' provided her a mood booster, as my student "changed the channel in her brain" to being ready to learn that morning. (Morin)

Complimenting a learner's appearance or personality might leave a child feeling temporarily great; but, teachers who can deliver specific positive feedback about a child's character, skills, and strengths can immeasurably inspire futuristic and life-altering purposes rooted in deep internal motivation.

Reinforcers through relationships.

 Expectations: Moving students from extrinsic motivation to having intrinsic motivation.

 Stuff: Intrinsic Motivation vs. Extrinsic Motivations

 Skills: Students are able to be self-aware of their own strengths.

Instruction/Activities:

There is an age old debate in our schools of whether or not we should be using extrinsic motivations. When I first started teaching, I distinctly recall another very well respected teacher who said that I should NEVER be giving kids rewards. She believed that rewards sent the wrong message and that they need to be internally driven. Furthermore, she explained how I was just feeding into really bad habits and they just needed to figure it out for themselves. She's partly right you know. An overreliance on extrinsic rewards can help extinguish internal drive.

"If you reward something, you get more of it. You punish something, you get less of it."
- Daniel Pink

This has stuck with me, and I am constantly thinking of ways to balance the two reward systems. Obviously, I agree that students need to be intrinsically motivated; but, it is not as simple as saying, "just do it because you want to." We have to find ways to balance the two types of motivation and help them see what intrinsic motivation can look and feel like. Internal drive is reinforced when teachers provide opportunities to pursue joyful learning. Joyful learning avoids obligations and compliance. Instead, it's led by passion filled projects which allows students to infuse the best parts of themselves into their work.

One of the top 5 motivators for learners is hearing someone use their name in a positive and welcoming way. We all love when other people pronounce our name correctly. We're actually wired to recognize and distinguish the sound of our name from other words. Names help us feel seen, valued, and connected to something bigger than ourselves. This is such a simple concept, but if you say a child's name when you are talking to them they are much more likely to work for you and be motivated.

I think about the student with "cool shoes" often and how she was motivated to work for me from such an offhand seemingly insignificant comment. How does this apply to all of the other interactions I have with students?

When we talk to students it's critical to reinforce what they are good at, improving at, or already accomplished at. This all goes back to relationships, relationships, relationships. You have to understand your students in order to help them become intrinsically motivated. Here's a few prompts:

You are Really good at...

You are better at ... than I am, can you help me.

I would Really appreciate it if you helped me with ..., you are so great at it.

When you write you have an amazing way of...

Let's do the math, Sammy, you are great at math, can you calculate this for us?

I love seeing all of your artwork on your assignments, would you be able to create a drawing for me, you have such a great eye for art.

You have a great way with words, will you explain this to Jaimie for me?

Obviously, this has to be genuine or your students will disregard your compliment. If you ask a student to draw something for you when they are only good at stick figures, they will see right through you and know you are not being real with them. Instead, play to their strengths. For example, I have had students over the years that are exceptionally organized and always kept their binders looking immaculate. Sometimes I'll have another student that has a binder that rivals a pig pen, dripping lost papers and metal rings about to explode from the tension of keeping it all together. I love capitalizing on these organized students' skills to help an organizationally challenged peer.

Praising a child's character reinforces positive behavior more than praising behavior. As organizational psychologist, Adam Grant, points out: "When our character is praised, we internalize it as part of our identity."

Using specific language with a learner helps reinforce a positive trait I see inside of them. The organized child always thrives on it and teaches the student how to organize and help them to keep it that way. They are definitely in their element. However, the follow-up with this is that I now have to become more committed than ever to make sure that my unorganized student doesn't think that I am picking on them, by helping them identify their character and personality strengths and how they can help others as well. I must see how they might serve and support our class ecosystem. A great way for teachers to identify these potential strengths is to ask students a simple question: What's one thing you could teach me how to do? This pointed inquiry can help us pinpoint follow-up questions that uncover a student's hidden talent.

> TEACHERS WHO ONLY IDENTIFY STRENGTHS IN A COUPLE STUDENTS FOSTER A TEACHER'S PET CULTURE THAT LEAVES OTHER STUDENTS FEELING ISOLATED AND UNSEEN.

Another example is that I have had some very dramatic actors in my classroom. They love to be on the stage and they are constantly disrupting my class with monologues about whatever our subject is at the time. I enjoy harnessing their talent for performance by asking them if they can read aloud to the class a novel, article, textbook, whatever we are learning at the time. This gives them the outlet to express their amazing skills as an actor and the class benefits from their dramatic reading of the material. Want to take it a step further? Let them stand up and move about the room. Giving them regular opportunities to shine in their performance helps them stay with you, during other more mundane class activities. Furthermore, if you're actually picking the right student(s) for this opportunity, I'll bet you that your entire class will be more engaged. Afterall, performance is this student's passion and talent for a reason. Witnessing someone (in this case a dramatic student reading) who is literally living out their why is inspiring to all observers.

- You have a very athletic student in your class, have them run the exercise breaks during work time.
- You have a great artist, have them create a diagram to be used as an example in class.
- You have an amazing writer, have them create an announcement to be read aloud.
- You have a student that loves to help others, have them ensure everyone has the supplies they need for an activity.
- You have an incredible rapper, encourage them to freestyle the outcome of cell mitosis.

Playing to a learner's individual strengths helps them to understand what they are talented at and how they can use those skills for good; while simultaneously becoming a powerful reward for the entire class. Kids that are given the chance to let their personality shine through are more likely to develop great character traits as they can match them to their personality.

 ## Close Intentionally:

I guarantee you're already providing intentional rewards and reinforcers occasionally with some students. However, in order to tap into our students' potential, we must connect with them in such a personalized way as to not miss all the obvious awesomeness inside of them. Teachers who truly have a relationship with each and every learner ensure their own ability to uncover the internal buttons.

> ARMED WITH A MAP OF OUR LEARNERS' MOTIVATIONAL DRIVERS, TEACHERS HAVE THE KEY TO HELP THEM UNLOCK SUSTAINABLE JOY.

Joy comes from understanding one's purpose. Can your learners each answer the following question:

'My purpose in this classroom is_____"

 ## Opportunities:

Classroom Jobs--this is common in a lot of elementary classrooms, as I remember having them when I taught in the lower grades. These should not just be randomly assigned. It's critical to match a job to a student's passion and purpose. These class roles help to intrinsically motivate students to work on their character by developing self-esteem and self-awareness around an intra-personal strength. The student that holds the door should be one that thrives off of smiling at others and helping them in some small way. The line leader should be someone who likes to take control of a situation and lead people with respect. These are all things that can inherently build opportunities for a student to practice working on one's own character.

While we all need to actively work on character and social emotional skills in which we struggled with, a strength based approach allows students to reach soft skill competence through a familiar successful learning pathway. Thus, I might be great at handing out smiles and kindness but struggle with patience. Of course, not every student who walks through the doorway will exhibit reflective kindness back to me. Their interactions might directly challenge my patience and commitment to serve them each day. Naturally, holding the door for peers will test my patience even while reinforcing my internal strength of kindness.

High School students need the same individual motivation, but you are now harnessing these skills to benefit them in life. This is where you use their strengths to heighten their learning. If they are an amazing artist then allow them to use those skills to express themselves and their learning. For their science project it might result in a visual display instead of a report. If you have students that have theatrical talent, maybe you have them do an interactive presentation for their science project as they actually perform the experiment in front of everyone. A student who's good with their hands might physically build something cool for the class to watch or observe.

Think you don't have enough jobs for all the students in your class?

Award Winning Classrooms realize that the number of roles that support a class are only limited by the number of students. Every student is in your class to support the entire group in some special way. Each learner is in YOUR ROOM for a reason.

> ## It's the teacher's job to help discover WHY a learner has been assigned to their classroom.

 **Needs:**

Teachers will know when rewards/reinforcers are beginning to work when they have students that are intrinsically motivated to do something amazing. For instance, the student who was cleaning the binder came to me and said that they saw someone with a messy locker and they wanted to stay in at lunch and help the other student clean it. Or you have the dramatic reader wanting to help someone else that is struggling to read. This is becoming a part of who they are and their character is shining through based on intrinsic rewards.

There's no greater reward than to watch students finding their joy in and out of your classroom.

 **Self-Reflection:**

What are ways that you can intrinsically motivate YOUR students?

Think about a few students that you have in your class, what is their personality, gifts, and strengths...AND how might you reinforce their awesomeness to help them tap into their own skills?

What ways will you make your classroom rewards inclusive for all students?

How does self-identified skill recognition help to motivate them internally?

How are you intrinsically motivated by your own life lessons?

Share out your reflections using #InspiringJY

AFFIRMATIONS

(Write, Draw, or Brainstorm ideas or thoughts here)

I am rewarding all learners if...

SEL is not anyone's responsibility - it's everyone's responsibility! Jennifer's LESSICONS provide all educators with real-life, easy to follow examples for how they can incorporate the whole learner in their academic content areas. Her passion for inspiring joy in students shines through in this book! After reading, you can't help but be **ENERGIZED** and **MOTIVATED** to immediately get back into the classroom and start making a difference.

Becky Thal, 5th Grade Teacher, Education Consultant

LESSON 5:

THROWN INTO THE FIRE—ACCOUNTABILITY

 Launch:

I grew up in the Pacific Northwest, and more specifically the State of Washington (aka Evergreen State.) We have beautiful mountains, lakes, rivers, and lush plants everywhere. When I was little, I learned to cast a line for fly fishing before I was able to bounce a basketball. My family loved the outdoors, so it is no surprise that we started camping when I was very young.

Our neighbor next door, Ann, happened to have a PhD in Geology and spent most of her life outdoors (I consider her a second mom). Ann's idea of luxury camping was having a fold out lounge chair to sleep under the stars. She knew a ton about camping, wilderness, and was our real-life tour guide to roughing it for many years.

Upon first going camping, we learned the basics about pitching a tent, starting a fire, cooking on the open flame, fishing, and hiking. We loved every minute of it! But it wasn't all rainbows and sunshine in the forest...

When I was 4 years old, I vividly remember one very overwhelming camping experience. In truth, almost every childhood camping memory is filled with warmth, fun, and joy. But unfortunately this one unforgettable event stands out for its sheer painful horror.

It was summertime in majestic Mt. Rainier. Growing up in the northwest, it's easy to get spoiled with the oxygen infused air and skyscraper trees. As is typical, it was beautifully refreshing each day but the temperature would often drop quite a bit at night. Thus, most early mornings would begin with hot cocoa as we sat around by the fire to warm up, before beginning our day of adventure.

One morning, my mom was so cold, she began warming herself up by the fire. She had her back turned to the fire and was wiggling her butt to warm up her back side. As we know, children often look toward their parents or other adults as a model of how to act.

42

And even the simplest action can look like magic through the eyes of a child. Naturally a few minutes later, I emulated my mom and began to warm my butt next to the flame.

As a newbie camper, I spun around and invariably lost my balance. Apparently, my coordination wasn't quite as refined as my mom's. Inevitably, I fell backwards into the white hot fire pit. My dad had built such a robust fire that my tumble sent burning embers flying everywhere.

Luckily for me, I was wearing lots of clothes, so I had a relatively thick layer of armored protection to burn through before it got to my skin. That being said, I was still too young to understand what to do next. Because I knew I needed to get up quickly, I reached out and grabbed the circular metal around the fire to help push myself up. Well, as experienced campers know, the metal ring helps trap all the flames, heat, and soot into one concentrated space. Needless to say that ring was searingly hot. As my butt's literally on fire, and I've burned my hands, I quickly struggle to dig my way out of the fire.

Keep in mind this all occurred in only a few seconds. My mom and Ann were quick to respond, as they grabbed the water bucket we had used for the dishes and dunked me butt first into the bucket. Thanks to the cold temperature outside, we still had ice in our cooler. As they flew around the campsite grabbing ice to put on my wounds immediately, the pain was beginning to set in.

I was lucky to have been wearing many layers as it somewhat protected my skin. However, sadly, they found out later, I had second degree burns on my finger tips, palms, and my butt. Blisters formed pretty quickly on my hands and bottom. [Ironically, even now as an adult I have poor fingerprint recognition and struggle to swipe and use newer phones. On a side note, I almost didn't become a teacher because I couldn't get my fingerprints to show up for my educator background check. They actually had to call in a CSI specialist to get my fingerprints to register because of the burns I suffered as a child].

While all of this campfire melee was going on, my dad was having an unusual, dare I say...out of character response. It's important that you know I'm a daddy's girl. He's the kindest most gentle person you can meet as he spent his life being my educational hero. He's a true servant leader who consistently puts his needs aside to help and support others. He's the guy you want by your side in a crisis. And even now as an adult I look up to and admire this retired educator more than almost anyone else in my life. But on this day, so many years ago, he was not his best self. Knowing my dad, he'd probably want a redo on his reaction...

While mom and Ann were whisking around tending to my needs, my dad was visibly angry at me for putting out his fire. He raised his voice and expressed disappointment toward me. As an adult, I understand his frustration that morning was probably more directed at himself out of fear and worry over my wellbeing. But, it sure felt like I disappointed him. Even now, as silly as it sounds, I still feel a little shame about falling in that fire.

My parents assessed the situation after I was all cooled off and decided that we would continue the camping trip. A visit to the doctor could wait as we let the wounds heal up on their own. In fact, my painful burns didn't deter our family from going on our planned hike. You should know, I was a total trooper! Moments like this probably taught me the grit to overcome horrible pain. And in many ways, this perseverance through pain, foreshadowed my life in ways that I'll share later in this book. To be honest though, I didn't hike most of it. My mom carried me almost all of the way because I was in so much pain and crying from the burns. Occasionally, she would stop and put my hands in the ice cold river to help relieve the burns. My parents had a detailed plan for our weekend and my accident wasn't going to deter them from accomplishing the family fun we desired.

As an adult now, I do NOT look back at this experience with anger, sadness or pain. Instead, as a veteran educator, I've sought out the lesson within the turmoil. Those quick to criticize, might question my parents supervision at that moment or their diligence to intentionally teach me how to warm my butt. But the truth is, stuff happens. And sometimes despite our best intentions children stumble and fall.

As a teacher, how do you handle student failure? Do you use it as a teachable moment? Are you quick to move on without mastery learning?

Sometimes life has a way of burning us...

> ## Joyful classrooms are led by teachers who take accountability for student stumbles.

Thrown into the Fire!

 Expectations: Educators need to use self-reflection to analyze a lesson/unit and look for ways to infuse JOY.

 Stuff: Accountability through Self-Reflection.

 Skills: When you are practicing accountability for you and your students, you will create an environment where your students will be self-aware, learn to self-manage, be socially aware, work on relationship skills, and use responsible decision making skills.

Instruction/Activities:

Do you blame your students for failure?

Or do you see failure as the first step toward learning?

Obviously, blaming a 4 year old for falling in a fire, is a mistake; but, many of us are making a similar mistake in our classrooms. Sometimes we arrive at the end of a unit and discover our students have performed poorly on the big test. Truthfully, we may have missed indicators of expected failure well before the assessment. Long before assessment ends, accountability begins.

PRACTICE

accountability

P re-assessment

R elationships

A uthentic feedback

C lass confusion

T hrow out the pacing guide

I - statements

C ollaboration

E ver-changing

P: Pre-Assessment

In the fire story, my parents would have been smart to do a quick check on my skills around the fire. As a teacher, our students show up to us with a variety of prior knowledge, experience, and self-efficacy. Taking the time to better understand the young people we hope to inspire ultimately informs award winning teaching.

R: Relationships

Sitting with a learner and having them explain the way they solve a math problem or construct an argumentative essay, provides educators an in depth examination of how to support the learner. Perhaps, my parents might have had me demonstrate how to behave next to a pretend fire at home, before we even left for our camping trip.

> FAILURE SHOULDN'T BE A GOTCHA BUT INSTEAD A CHANCE TO SAY I GETCHA-
> -MEANING I UNDERSTAND YOUR THINKING!

Seeking personal feedback from your students allows us to uncover what they are having trouble with. By teaching them how to give specifics, I have my students take me through the steps and then show me where they are stumbling. This can pinpoint errors and really get to the root of the problem.

One time, I had a math student who was really struggling with balancing equations. He'd try and try but continued to fail. Finally, he showed me the steps he had taken and couldn't get past this one step. As it turned out, he didn't know his multiplication table so he wasn't able to multiply and divide because he didn't have the basic knowledge. Listening to him helped me pinpoint where the breakdown occurred. Had I simply continued to reteach and reteach him this same balancing, that poor kid would have never gotten it. And his frustrations probably would have spilled into behavior, low motivation, and poor self-efficacy.

Instead, I provided him with a multiplication chart and the use of a calculator, so that he didn't get stuck in the weeds, while he was solving more complicated problems. Additionally, I personalized his entry tasks to start embedding multiplication practice as a warm up to our daily work. Over time, his confidence grew and he avoided the need to step back entirely from more complicated problem solving because I listened closely to him.

A: Authentic Feedback

Educators must give students an opportunity to share their learning without being caught up in a grade. And technology has given innovative educators so many quick and easy check points of student understanding. By providing regular formative assessments, we ensure that students don't wind up getting burned, at the end of a unit.

EMAIL, DM, PRIVATE MESSAGE, COMMENT ON PAPER are all easy examples of how to gain authentic feedback from students.

C: Class Confusion

Have you ever had multiple students, start asking the same question. We often assume that students aren't listening when you answer it the first time. But the truth is, students ask questions when they don't 'get it.' And 'not getting it' is a sign that as educators we need to hold ourselves accountable to reteaching, in a different way. This is not the time to roll your eyes at the duplicity of inquiry and repeat your same answer. In fact, students are given the gift of being interested in learning. Take this opening and share a new example, idea, or way of thinking about their question.

If they were off task; it wasn't engaging. If they were bored; it wasn't a high enough level of content. If they kept saying they didn't understand; it might be too high of content. If they kept making mistakes; it wasn't intentionally taught.

T: Throw out the Pacing Guide

Most pacing guides allow teachers to hit SOME of the students. At best pacing guides allow teachers to hit MOST of our students. Which is why schools, districts and individual educators are moving toward self-paced mastery or personalized learning. The thought that a district led pacing chart will work for all the students sitting in your classroom is short-sided, archaic...and flat out WRONG!

> *"When we discuss the need for personalization of education but then try to create standardized outcomes for all students, the notion of personalization becomes moot."*
> *- George Couros, Innovate Inside the Box*

I: I-Statements

Using I-Statements forces teachers to look in the mirror when reflecting on a plan, instruction, or assessment. When we talk through an I-lens we're able to avoid finger pointing that typically devolves into blaming a particular class, previous teacher, or other barriers to student learning. My dad who is one of the most patient people I've ever met lost his temper with me for putting out this beautiful fire he had built. When in reality he was frustrated with himself because he knew the situation could have been prevented had intentional teaching happened before I fell. Using an I-Statement would have helped him avoid blame and shame.

As an educator, I only have control over my actions. However, as teachers we are one of the most important and powerful leaders our students will ever encounter. We have tremendous influence and leverage over making tiny changes that facilitate learning. These changes might take the form of instruction, classroom setting, lesson design, etc.. But they can only happen if my energy, focus, and attention is centered around a self-focused question: how might I improve my teaching TODAY?

> *"Better Today than Yesterday.*
> *Better Tomorrow than Today."*
> *Teach Better Team*

C: Collaboration

PLC's , PLN, parent/teacher communication, and student/teacher conferencing can all provide incredible information to lead accountability. When we're willing to be vulnerable and share what's not working with others and then deeply listen to feedback and response, this coordinated effort to improve the learning experience can have astronomical impact. I think teachers often feel like they have to be the experts of their room.

> JOY FILLED CLASSROOMS ARE CONNECTED CLASSROOMS.

Educators in these environments realize that others can make them better. Thus, they are willing to turn over any and all stakeholder stones in the pursuit of a better student experience.

E: Ever-changing

> *"Change the game, don't let the game*
> *change you."*
> *-Macklemore*

Our world is changing so fast. In his book *Future Driven*, Geurin points out that we need to raise, teach, and support flexible learners, in order to prepare them for an ever changing workplace. Thankfully, student brains have the capacity for adaptational growth because of neuroplasticity.

[Neuroplasticity, also known as neural plasticity, or brain plasticity, is the ability of neural networks in the brain to change through growth and reorganization. These changes range from individual neurons making new connections, to systematic adjustments like cortical remapping]
(Doidge, 2007)

BUT HERE'S A LITTLE SECRET, PLASTICITY OF LEARNING ALSO IMPLIES PLASTICITY OF TEACHING.

No two class dynamics are ever the same. No two students are ever the same. What worked this year in AP Science may not work next year. Staying flexible allows educators to adapt, shift, and meld their teaching plan to fit the ever changing learner and world. Covid-19 taught us that you have to be prepared to change instantly in some cases and adapt to new settings for education.

 ## Close Intentionally:

How will YOU remember to PRACTICE Accountability?

Building reflection into your lesson design might be a healthy way to start developing your accountability muscle. I literally include a spot in my lesson plan book to jot insights, I-statements, and takeaways so that I can assess, alter, and amplify my lesson. Don't wait until the end of the unit or worse yet school year to make adjustments. Alterations should be made on the fly, throughout the day. If something bombed in your first class of the day, it would be ridiculous to continue for the rest of the day with the same exact plan. Having a spot to reflect, in real time, forces me to hold myself accountable to the flexibility of mind that Geurin so eloquently supports.

As you start getting more comfortable with holding yourself accountable, you can infuse self-reflection into your PLC process (Little and McLaughlin), PLN, parent conferences, teacher evaluations, professional growth plans, and student conferencing. You might even literally write the words PRACTICE accountability on the back wall of your classroom as a visual reminder to stay focused on a growth mindset! Being mindful of self-improvement is a beautiful model for our students.

Opportunities:

How might my own parents have differentiated our camping experience? Perhaps, they would have pre-taught me some fire safety. Or even after falling in the fire, maybe my dad would have taken my brother on a hike while someone stayed back with me to heal up and learn appropriateness near the fire.

As teachers, we usually have a plan for our instruction that can last one week, one unit, or even an entire year. We tell ourselves that we're not doing our job, if we don't stick to this original plan. And this negative self-talk is supported and reinforced by outside district, building, and grade level forces. We fear deviation from perfectly drawn up recipes of learning so when things don't go as planned we start blaming others rather than naming solutions--SHAME!

> *"Shame corrodes the very part of us that believes we are capable of change."*
> -Brené Brown

We have an opportunity to model empathy and growth for our colleagues when we sidestep shame and lean in to malleable instruction.

 ## Needs:

How do you know you followed through with Accountability?

One big sign of successful classroom accountability is that you rarely find yourself sticking to your exact lesson plan. If we're listening to ourselves and others then we are probably constantly tweaking EVERYTHING we're doing to meet students where they are by remaining flexible leaders.

Also, stakeholders start offering up helpful feedback that we actually are attuned to. When educators create accountable classrooms, they seek ways to improve from any and everybody. They stop viewing themselves as the classroom experts and instead know that the smartest person in the room is the ACTUAL ROOM! And guess what...the ROOM starts speaking it's brilliance on how to make learning AWARD WINNING!

When our colleagues, parents, and students know that we truly hold ourselves accountable they also begin to raise their accountability game.

How different is a parent teacher conference where the teacher points out their own mistakes and class failures to a parent rather than simply offering a greatest hits behavioral run down of how little Johnny is misbehaving in social studies? Modeling accountability leads to others holding themselves more accountable.

 **Self-Reflection:**

When's the last time you threw YOUR students into the 'fire'?

What percentage of the class is acceptable failure?

What's one way you'll begin to hold yourself more ACCOUNTABLE this week?

When is a time in your life that you fell into a fire? What did you learn?

Share out your reflections using #InspiringJOY

AFFIRMATIONS

(Write, Draw, or Brainstorm ideas or thoughts here)

I hold myself accountable by ...

As educators around the world continue to examine, adapt, and redefine what teaching and learning should look like post-COVID. Jennifer Appel offers an **INGENIOUS** method to increase our intentionality regarding infusing best-practices into each and every lesson. *Inspiring Joy* offers a just-in-time framework which will transform the approach educators take when planning and implementing instruction daily. It's revolutionary, **TRANSFORMATIVE**, and a powerful resource which will serve as a guide for any teacher, instructional coach, or school leader looking to increase student outcomes and elevate instructional practice.

**Jami Fowler-White, Educator, Author, Poet,
and Founder/CEO of Digital PD 4 You**

LESSON 6:

BRONCO II - COMMON LANGUAGE

🚀 Launch:

When I was in early elementary school my family spent Thanksgiving with my grandparents who lived in this cute little bavarian town called Leavenworth. We lived about 3 hours away across a small mountain pass. Having gone to their house for the holiday during a wintry mix , we were eager to get on our way home the next day before the roads got too icy.

During our drive, the weather was increasingly cold and a little snowy, but we had a Ford Bronco II and it had four wheel drive so my parents figured we were good to go. Unfortunately, overnight the roads had caked over with black ice, so my dad had no idea they were completely covered with slick patches. And as luck would have it, we hit a really bad stretch of black ice and our car went spinning around. [If you're a car aficionado you'll recall the old Bronco II's from the 80's had a very high center of gravity. Which is probably why they were all built with roll bars].

After hitting this bad patch of road, the car started to lose control. Being out of control can be a terrifying feeling! Our car twisted with such speed and force that at one point the car flipped over. Sitting upside down against an embankment on the side of the road, I was filled with shock. Like an unwilling participant on a roller coaster of fear, I will always remember the trauma of that ordeal.

But the real life lesson had less to do about driving conditions, safety, and ice and more to do with communication. After landing against the embankment, I vividly remember my dad yelling: "***GAS***!!"

With no time to spare my dad and mom communicated instantly about the need to hustle and get everyone out of the car immediately from this one simple word. As a unified team operating out of the same panic stricken playbook, both mom and dad had instant recognition that the car might very well explode because of leaking fuel. There was no time for verbal family check-in to ensure everyone was ok. Instead, action was needed.

(53)

Years removed, I stand in wonder how my dad's single word "GAS" triggered such rapid response from my mom. Cleary my dad thought with the roll of the car and hitting the embankment we had perforated the gas tank. He thought that he smelled gas and the car could catch on fire. My parents knew each other so well and had such a powerful common language that uttering a single word resulted in a quick teamwork of action.

In our classrooms, the stakes might feel less intense than that icy day in late November; but, creating joy-filled classrooms that have life-altering consequences means the ability to utilize a common language is no less important. The best teachers often speak a learning language that's so universally understood by all stakeholders that inspiring actionable kindness, empathy, and service are a beautiful byproduct.

> ### Joyful classrooms bestow teachers a common language that supports rich character development.

Common language creates a safe environment to teach and learn.

 Expectations: Students need to understand what everything means in your classroom and beyond, by making sure you are on the same page as your colleagues and your school/district.

 Stuff: District, school-wide, grade level, and classroom common language.

 Skills: By using common language with students they are able to be self-aware and self-manage their own behavior and actions through responsible decision making.

Instruction/Activities:

Before you begin teaching your students common language make sure that you are in agreement with your grade level teammates, hallway, and your school. Students need to have consistency and hear the same message from everyone in the school. Common Language should become part of the vernacular in your classroom. Our overarching pillars in an Award Winning Culture are Character, Excellence, and Community. Those 3 words are used constantly when we are talking to students, parents, and staff not only about behavior but when we are discussing curriculum, events, projects, flexible seating, etc.. They are in consistent use to remind everyone how they can show Character, Excellence and Community in simple attainable ways.

- But using common language goes beyond students, and must be expressed to families, co-workers, and the community.
  - During parent teacher conferences, the 3 overarching ideas are within the structure of the discussion. For example, how are your students doing their best? We can then provide tangible examples of where those are showing up in their work and classroom behavior. What are they doing for others today? That is showing up here, in what they are doing for this student, or how they are serving the school. You are constantly using the common language in every situation that comes up at school. How are they doing the right thing in and out of my class? Citing specific examples of student character is a wonderful gift to share with parents.
  - When you are talking to colleagues about a student, use common language to help figure out a plan and as a driving force for decision making. This can be used in many ways to help you narrow your focus and keep your own purpose and school's mission at the forefront of decisions.
  - When you are posting on your readerboard, make sure you are using common language that you want to infuse into the community. Try to always have these words embedded into posters and publicity about school events.
- Another example of this happens when you are having a problem in your hallway, grade level, or school.
  - Before you start talking to your class about it, find out what other teachers in the hallway and grade level are seeing and hearing. Collaborating with other teachers and admin gives us a sense for the problem and the vocabulary to address it.
  - Talking to my team is always a top priority. This gives me a chance to come up with a solution, time to talk with our students, and a clear message to deliver to the learners.
  - After that we send an email to the admin communicating to them what we are observing, how we handled it, and how they could use the same language when they were talking to students. It is consistent and everyone understands what the issues are and they are all getting the same clear message.
  - Next, we communicate with parents either through email, video, letter, or messaging service about the observed behavior and expected correction. This ensures parents have the correct story, language, and information to follow up at home.
  - Finally, sharing feedback with our students on how the behavior has improved. (this is OFTEN overlooked). Put a voice to the positive effort you're noticing!
  - Example: "Thank you so much, I have seen high CHARACTER this week from all of you. You are DOING THE RIGHT THING by walking in the hallway and keeping your hands to yourself."

Close Intentionally:

When thinking of common language make sure to use all aspects of the student's day, not just during times of rules and discipline. By embedding the language in everything happening in the classroom, it will become second nature for you and your students. Thus, a huge pitfall to avoid is only using desired character focused language when correcting behavior. Great teachers talk about school-wide ideas like character traits, branding, and social emotional skills during all times. Here's a couple examples:

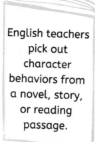

English teachers pick out character behaviors from a novel, story, or reading passage.

History teacher facilitates debate on empathy's role in the fall of the roman empire, holocaust, or civil war.

Music teacher shares how students practice servant leadership by helping a classmate set up their stands, music, instrument, etc.

PE teacher emphasizes sportsmanship by picking out best teammate awards for students who lift others up.

Science teacher talks about showing kindness and empathy toward your classmates by following lab safety procedures.

 ## Opportunities:

Sometimes I hear teachers saying that my kids aren't old enough, sophisticated enough, or mature enough to understand the language. My response with students is to start pre-teaching that relates directly to their level. All students can be exposed to sophisticated language. They simply need some context in explaining what that language means and how it relates to them. Students learn sophisticated language—the more you use it. Using the language in context significantly accelerates student growth. And by all means-- highlight, praise, and celebrate when learners use common language themselves!

 ## Needs:

You will know when your students, parents, and community are learning common language when they use it back to you. I have had parents using Character, Excellence, and Community when discussing something with their child. It's so exciting to hear these reassuring messages parroted back to me through multiple layers of translation. This school-wide verbiage is far reaching when we're all using, rewarding, and highlighting it consistently.

 **Self-Reflection:**

What common language would you like to see in your classroom?

How can you express these words to others in your hallway, grade level, subject area? How can you express these to parents and community?

How can you ensure that your school's common language is understood across all culturally diverse groups?

Life lessons can give us our own common language, what is a word in your family that has a special, well understood meaning?

Share out your reflections using #InspiringJOY

AFFIRMATIONS

(Write, Draw, or Brainstorm ideas or thoughts here)

Common Language in my classroom is taught when I...

After 20+ years of teaching, what I have learned about teaching the whole child from Jennifer Appel is inspiring and makes me a better teacher every single day. The ideas are **EASY TO IMPLEMENT** and have changed the culture in my classroom and at school. I wish I had this inspiration from day one. THANK YOU!
Michelle Thompson, 8th grade ELA teacher

LESSON 7:

PERSONALIZED DEVELOPMENT - TRAINING

 Launch:

Paul Dowdy was an outstanding educator. He moved impressively from teacher to building administrator in short order. He would go on to inspire generations of students, staff, and families through his work as a state recognized award winning principal. For 30 years, the West Richland community looked up to Mr. Dowdy as the educational leader.

But for me, he was just...Dad.

After retiring from public education, dad would go on to spend the next 15 years with my mom running Heritage University's educational program. In addition to handling all aspects of registration, advisory, and heading the educational department, my dad taught teacher prep classes for years.

After earning my masters in literacy, I set my sights on pursuing a dream of mine to teach a few college classes to future educators. I applied and was accepted to be an adjunct professor and teach education courses. Soon after, my dad approached me and asked if maybe we could team teach some classes together. As a newbie, this seemed like a good idea to help get my feet wet in the profession. We began teaching classes that focused on pedagogy, lesson planning, classroom management, and the fundamentals of creating an award winning classroom. I loved teaching these classes with my dad because we had such different perspectives within the same profession. He was an elementary principal and I was a middle school teacher. The dichotomy of educational insight was both vast and deep.

Needless to say, we didn't always agree on everything that was shared. I would disagree with what he said and he would do the same for me. It was a wonderful checks and balance that offered new educators a peek behind the school curtain. We had a healthy and respectful banter back and forth, as we took class discussions to a whole new level. Students would usually lean forward and enjoy the show while they interjected a question to keep the lively debate going for a while. They learned so much from our different viewpoints on the same issue. I remember students years later who would come back and tell us that they learned so much in our classes. They always appreciated these authentic conversations. Additionally, students loved that education didn't have one answer. One could be a great teacher and have a completely different spin on the same idea.

> ### EDUCATION IS NOT BLACK AND WHITE...AND OFTENTIMES THE EXCEPTIONAL CLASSROOM EXPERIENCES ARE FOUND IN THE GREY.

Having spent 45 years in education, dad is now retired and enjoying time with his grandchildren, fly fishing, reading, doing wood work, and many other hobbies. Reflecting back on my gift of classroom instruction time with him, I'm proud that we both found ways to infuse ourselves into the work. Rather than creating a derivative or watered down stance on classrooms we opted to stay true to ourselves in the same vein that Kris Felicello and Gary Armida write from in *The Teacher and The Admin*. It's critical for teachers to seek ongoing learning that's inspiring and helps us grow. However, as I talked about in Lesson 1, we must not throw-out all our prior knowledge and experience when beginning something new.

> ### JOYFUL EDUCATORS DIVERSIFY THEIR PROFESSIONAL DEVELOPMENT TO GAIN GREATER UNDERSTANDING OF THE CURRICULUM.

Extensive training so that you understand how to teach the concept with fidelity.

 Expectations: Use educational cross-training to learn as much about an idea before you implement it into your classroom.

 Stuff: Varied Trainings through diversified professional development.

 Skills: Students will learn that training will help them to use social awareness and relationship skills into adulthood.

Instruction/Activities:

When learning a new idea or concept for your classroom or your school [including character development] always consider the ways you can expand your thinking into creative avenues which can tap into more information and cross-training that expand your professional development. When we first obtained our current SEL curriculum CharacterStrong, I loved it from the moment that I saw it. John Norlin and Houston Kraft do an amazing job of creating lessons that are powerful and entertaining for students. While I loved the curriculum, I knew that I needed to learn more about the theory behind it. I knew its creators had based a lot of their work on James Hunter's bestselling book: *The Servant*; thus, I started looking into Hunter to uncover what his ideas were all about. I read 3 of his books to learn the foundation for which our new curriculum came from. It helped me to see the ideas from a different perspective.

> HAVING BREADTH AND DEPTH OF BACKGROUND KNOWLEDGE CAN SUPPORT EDUCATORS' DESIRE TO BREAK CONCEPTS DOWN FOR OUR STUDENTS.

Understanding Hunter's focus on supporting business leaders through servant leadership helped me to conceptualize how character development applies to the workforce when students graduate. Putting the curriculum into perspective gave me a long term vision for my students. The ability to see the big picture in our classroom and beyond allows a teacher to establish a more inspiring destination than simply a test, unit, or grade level completion. After reading Hunter's work, I was introduced to Simon Sinek's ideas on creating these purposeful work environments for businesses. I began to learn how teaching students to discover and develop their why would lead them to live more joyful lives. Again, this proved to be a powerful way to train my brain outside of education.

Award Winning Culture refers to this style of educational professional development as cross training. Educators must look at content from multiple angles. How does your science instruction fit in with ELA content? How might you support health curriculum in a STEM or physical education course. What is the relationship between my math class and my students' previous or future social studies classes.

> SOLVING THE EDUCATIONAL PUZZLE MEANS UNDERSTANDING HOW ALL THE K-12 SCHOOL PIECES FIT TOGETHER.

There's a body of research to support school culture through content homogeneous Professional Learning Communities. However, some of the best training occurs from collaboration outside one's immediate content area. These cross curricular moments can even filter down to student experience. Planning a lesson that extends into multiple content classes ensures students are provided a lens of how and why concepts fit together. For example, an ELA teacher might help support the research and technical writing skills necessary to help learners bring a biological experiment into fruition in their science class.

Content connection yields relevance and educational relevance supports internal purpose.

This helps us explain to students the outside ramifications of this work and how it will help them in the long run...RELEVANCE! When you are examining training, don't just focus on the obvious ways of learning. Instead, intentionally take a look at outside sources that show you the big picture of the idea or concept that will give you and your learners more perspective.

 ## Close Intentionally:

When you are thinking about teaching an SEL and/or character curriculum, understand the concept at its core and supplement educational cross training to expand your learning. 93% of teachers surveyed by Civic Enterprises said that they want a "greater focus on SEL" and other whole learner content in schools (Casel.org) but understanding where to start can feel exhausting...

Do you ever feel completely overwhelmed by the amount of educational jargon coming at you? To make sense of all the important training pieces for teachers, I've created the following graphic to support an award winning mindset.

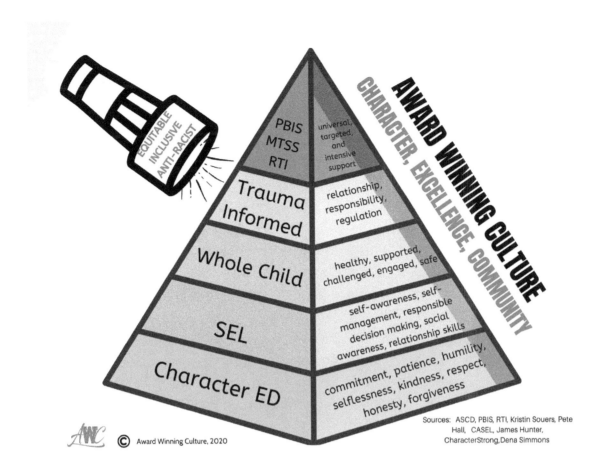

On the pyramid:

PBIS MTSS RTI — universal, targeted, and intensive support

Trauma Informed — relationship, responsibility, regulation

Whole Child — healthy, supported, challenged, engaged, safe

SEL — self-awareness, self-management, responsible decision making, social awareness, relationship skills

Character ED — commitment, patience, humility, selflessness, kindness, respect, honesty, forgiveness

EQUITABLE INCLUSIVE ANTI-RACIST

AWARD WINNING CULTURE
CHARACTER, EXCELLENCE, COMMUNITY

Sources: ASCD, PBIS, RTI, Kristin Souers, Pete Hall, CASEL, James Hunter, CharacterStrong, Dena Simmons

In schools we must focus on character, SEL, whole child, trauma informed, PBIS, RTI, MTSS, and equity. But what do they all mean? Are they the same thing? Are they interchangeable? And most importantly--how they support one another. I created this graphic to explain how all of these elements relate and connect to one another and why they are so important to an Award Winning Culture.

At the bottom of the pyramid is character education, the character traits that we are teaching, supporting, and focusing on with our students. Depending on your curriculum or culture you have different traits you are teaching; but they really boil down to empathy, kindness, service and respect. For instance, it's critical for us to intentionally teach students how to show empathy, model kindness or practice service toward others. This is the WHY of an Award Winning Culture and it is absolutely the foundation of the entire pyramid.

Next, is SEL (social emotional learning)--which is the WHAT. It is what successfully prepared students look like (I.E self-awareness, self-management, etc. (CASEL)). It is WHAT the students are doing to show they understand their WHY. SEL is the specific actionable soft skills for teachers to focus on to support a holistic learner.

In today's education, we hear a lot about the whole child. We must understand and reach the whole child. Teachers nowadays know that being a classroom teacher goes well beyond the core content. Seeing the whole child is imperative to uncovering each learner's WHO. Who are we doing all of this for--the whole child! This is challenging kids, helping them to feel safe and supported. This is giving them the essentials they need to be a complete and WHOLE human being. The COVID-19 global pandemic reinforced that teachers must focus on the WHOLE LEARNER.

Educators who are trauma informed, help address the WHERE for their students. Where did they come from? Where have they been? Where do they need support? Three focus points by Kristin Souers and Pete Hall include: "relationships, responsibility, and regulation." These three aspects of supporting children of trauma are important to understand so we can help each student achieve their dreams and goals and ultimately get started toward their desired life path.

Sometimes, students need interventions, rewards or additional resources to provide them with access to a successful learning environment. At the top of the pyramid we identify WHEN they might need these supports. Depending on your building or district, you might refer to these supports as PBIS, MTSS, or RTI. This is WHEN the who, what, why, and where are getting their supports.

The scope of diversity provides teachers a lens to view school culture and climate through equity, inclusion, and anti-racism. This gives teachers the HOW to implement all of the pyramid in a culturally appropriate manner. Rather than seeing all students as the same and assuming every learner has similar opportunities and prior and current experiences, equity informs culturally responsive educators on how best to teach, intervene, model, and practice all the key elements on the pyramid. [If you want more information about equitable practices a great read is Zaretta Hammond's book Culturally Responsive Teaching and The Brain.]

> "If we can have policies and real education reform that gets at the most marginalized in our society then it will permeate to everyone else. If we're taking care of the most vulnerable...we're going to be able to make some real changes."
> -Bettina Love

How are you going to apply a lens of diversity to every situation in your school culture? What training would support your desire to inspire joy for EACH learner?

As with any pyramid if you are missing one layer, it will fall and crumble over time. But, remember that every pyramid was built one brick and one layer at a time. Take your time and build your pyramid to last. And when you have all of these elements you have created an Award Winning Culture in your school or classroom.

Teachers are constantly wearing different hats to keep the pyramid from crumbling. Thus, it's not good enough to focus our professional growth or teacher prep programs on instruction only. Nowadays, teachers need a diversified set of skills to reach their students.

♥ Opportunities:

When you are looking at incorporating a new idea in your classroom, peel back the multiple layers of perspective on the idea. Try to find ways to help you understand the concept at its core, not just what is being presented to you.

 ## Needs:

When you are able to explain the big ideas behind an initiative or idea at its core and truly believe in the work you are creating for students within your personal WHY; your lessons now have the opportunity to be exceptionally aligned with your daily work with learners.

 ## Self-Reflection:

How are you expanding your learning beyond just the education side of an idea?

Are you cross training when learning a new concept, idea or initiative?

What's one life lesson that taught you how to pause and really uncover the meaning behind it?

What part of the award winning culture diagram do you need additional training on? What's your plan to receive that professional development?

Share out your reflections using #InspiringJ🍎Y

AFFIRMATIONS

(Write, Draw, or Brainstorm ideas or thoughts here)

I AM EXPERIENCING INCREDIBLE PROFESSIONAL DEVELOPMENT WHEN...

In *Inspiring JOY*, author Jennifer Appel shares her passion for joyful learning with practical strategies any teacher can implement in the classroom. Emphasizing character, excellence, and community with personal stories of reflection, Jennifer's words create a path **ILLUMINATED** with light and joy. No matter what challenges come your way, *Inspiring JOY* will guide each step forward!

Tamara Letter, M.Ed., Instructional Coach, Technology Integrator, and Author of *A Passion for Kindness: Making the World a Better Place to Lead, Love, and Learn*

LESSON 8:

LIVE ON BROADWAY -EXPERIENTIAL

🚀 Launch:

> *"Forget regret, or life is yours to miss.*
> *No other path, no other way, no day but today."*
> -Jonathan Larson, Rent

I will never forget my first experience in New York. Being able to see a live Broadway production is a magical can't miss for out of towners. We've all watched theater on television or at the movies but until you actually experience the energy of a live (anything can happen) play or production, nothing can compare. When I was graduating from college with my masters degree, Hans asked me how I wanted to celebrate. No question, I wanted to go to New York!

I longed to see a musical called RENT. Rent is an amazing story of the year in the life of a group of artists struggling in modern day East Village New York. I had the CD (yes CD, this was before iTunes and music streaming in general) of the entire musical and loved listening to it. It had such a powerful message of love and understanding. Upon walking into this historic theater, near Times Square, one could feel the nervous excitement of the live audience as the incredible performers shared the electric songs that I'd played over and over. I can't even describe the feeling of seeing the live performance on this otherworldly wooden stage. I knew all of the words to every song sung and yet still sat in awe as if I was hearing them for the first time. The actors were so much more powerful on stage as we watched them glide around so beautifully. It literally took my breath away. While I'd heard the words many times through my stereo, the show reinforced to me how much more we can learn through experiential moments--doing and then reflecting on the doing.

I'm sure I hummed those show tunes for months as I reflected on a critical question: How could I bring this experience back to my classroom?

Successful teachers quickly recognize the value in students experiencing their learning. Rather than viewing SEL as something to tell students about, or to simply teach to learners...teachers can dig deeper and find experiential ways of reaching the whole child and beyond.

EdTeachers can infuse relevant character development and social emotional learning into core content by intentionally creating experiential project based learning moments.

Teaching character through project based learning.

 Expectations: Students need project based learning incorporated as much as possible in their learning experiences.

 Stuff: Character traits infused into project based learning.

 Skills: To make sure you are creating an authentic project based learning experience, make sure to incorporate all 5 skills, self-awareness, self-management, social awareness, relationship skills, and responsible decision making.

 Instruction/Activities:

"Tell me and I forget. Teach me and I remember. Involve me and I LEARN."
-Benjamin Franklin

Project based learning has been around for years, and we all know the value in this type of teaching and learning. One aspect that is not always talked about is how this builds character and how we need to intentionally teach character BEFORE PBL can begin. This pre-teaching not only helps projects to run smoother but ensures that the deeper learning connections can be reinforced. Project based learning is all about experiencing events for yourself, but you can only do that if you have the proper tools and skills to work together and demonstrate positive character in the process.

Before we start doing project based learning activities in our classrooms, we have to establish a core understanding of character. What does it mean to have award winning character? The question that we ask: Will you do the right thing? What does the 'right thing' look like in a classroom when you are working with others? How do students actually behave when doing the right thing?

Look at the House Rules section for examples on how to accomplish this brainstorming session.

Discussing with my class different ways to work together, has long been a staple of fostering class culture. It's critical to ensure everyone has a voice, by building student leaders, to help make decisions and lead discussions without overpowering peers. Educators must help students play to their strengths. If you have really bad handwriting, being the group secretary might not be the ideal role for you. At the very least, note taking might need to take the form of typing. Student's with artistic talents can take control of the visual direction of the project.

Providing opportunities for students to dable and reflect on their skills can help them to identify strengths and weaknesses within themselves. When starting projects, students are able to understand what they are good at and what they need from others. If students can strengthen their own identity and sense of self, it becomes much easier to group each other. When students have practice recognizing unique talents and skills in others, they're able to work cohesively and avoid many of the instances where tension arises within a group.

PEER EMPATHY LEADS TO GROUP INCLUSION.

Additionally, as a class, we discuss strategies for resolving conflict. Students create agreed upon solutions and norms for settling these issues. They might decide to have civil discourse, official voting, or use something like rock, paper, scissors to predetermine how they might handle challenges that surface. We always generate a list of strategies that they can use before any project begins. Whatever strategy works for a given group, works for me. Most importantly, students will be expected to self manage these moments of tension rather than quickly devolving into argument or seeking my intervention.

Lastly, they will need to decide on a vocal leader for the group that will speak to me if they are unable to resolve a conflict. Sometimes educators observe groups getting into disagreements and students struggle to explain the root of the problem to the teacher and end up all talking at the same time and not really telling you anything. Generally, when the teacher is unclear on the actual problem finding a workable solution can be challenging. Having one verbal representative who's able to articulate the concern ensures that the teacher will have the best information available to bring this group barrier to a close.

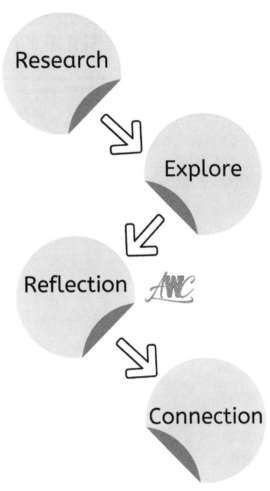

Research - Students watch videos, read books, articles and blogs, listen to podcasts and dig up information through reliable sources. Academic crafting, similar to a concept that organizational psychologists call Job crafting, is when teachers allow students to customize a passion project to fit their strengths, values, and interests as they become an active architect in designing their own learning.

Explore - Students are then given the opportunity to use the knowledge they gained to explore the idea with action. They create materials, write, experiment, test out, play with, express electronically or visually. Essentially they uncover a concept in greater detail by applying their research through CREATION.

Reflection - Most assignments stop after the exploring phase but reflection is where learning truly crystalizes. After exploring and experimenting with the concept they are able to reflect about what they learned. They can analyze an idea, creation, or exploration and see if it worked, or maybe there was something they had to adjust along the way. This form of critical thought invites authentic learning when students are able to synthesis the information and evaluate it from an open growth mindset.

> PROJECT BASED LEARNING IS NOT ABOUT BEING MISTAKE FREE...IT'S ABOUT ENCOURAGING STUDENTS TO DISCOVER THE EDGES OF POSSIBILITY.

Connection - Student connection to big ideas is revealed in a litany of different ways. One is that they are able to make connections through prior experiences with project based learning. They are able to look back and see what did and didn't work in previous projects. The second connection is with each other. Teamwork is powerful! The old saying is two brains are better than one. This really helps students to see things from a different perspective and learn how to gather all of the ideas and shape them into an amazing project.

 ## Close Intentionally:

Learners will reflect on their project and grade themselves from both a group lens and individual standpoint.

Whenever you do a group project it is much more reliable to ask the students how they did and what they might do differently next time. Exploring what was successful and areas of improvement provides learners with the privilege of practicing a growth mindset in a real world application. The best projects allow students to learn beyond content.

> *"Perhaps, academic content is just a vehicle to teach kids what matters most...character, excellence, and community."*
> *-Hans Appel, Award Winning Culture*

Opportunities:

Using multiple modalities during project based learning helps to capitalize on student strengths, which obviously fosters engagement. As a general rule, if educators are intentionally opting students out of group work, in favor of siloed assignments, an excellent character and social emotional learning experience might be missed. Of course, you will have those students that have a really hard time working in groups. They may have less experience, or limited interpersonal skills. Perhaps, no one wants to work with them and they have difficulties functioning with others.

> **However, students who struggle to work in a group are the ones that MOST NEED the opportunity to work in a group.**

We tend to let them work alone because it is easier for us--the teachers--as we worry that group challenges will impede academic learning for them and/or their peers. No, No, No-- they need this work the most and honestly they usually crave it the most, despite their words and actions to the contrary. While introverted students need some intentional individual time to work; project based learning that fails to be collaborative can feel very lonely at times.

Loneliness is the extent to which we attribute meaning to our social interactions; but one does not need to be physically by themselves to be lonely. The truth is, we can be alone in a crowd.

Fear usually leads to them putting an emotional or behavioral wall to effectively opt out of these important moments of growth. Teachers have to work harder with them to make sure they are getting what they need. We might need to help them identify their strengths and understand how they can contribute to the group. Perhaps, they are in the group but working on an independent aspect within the greater group like making pictures, building, researching, etc.. Next time, these learners can work with one other member of the group to accomplish their portion of the project. Gradually over time, they will be able to work with the entire group, as educators ease them into it. I also make sure I'm giving these students independent time to recharge their batteries. Remember--this may take some time! I've had students that weren't able to fully integrate into a group, until the very last project of the year. Whereas other students might be ready to be fully functioning group members in only a few months. Don't give up on them!

There is also a tremendous character benefit for the other students working in these groups. Imagine the opportunities to practice things like patience, empathy, selflessness, and respect. Working with someone who comes from a differing viewpoint, background, or skill set can feel maddening at times. But diversity of thought reinforces one's own character while establishing a setting for an overall better product. Imagine the projects that learners can create with a group all coming together from completely different angles. Imagine the world they might create in the future...

 ## **Needs:**

Let's examine one example of this type of PBL that I do with my 6th grade History class which is called 'Society Simulation'. Within the project students learn about ancient civilizations and the construction of the first societies. Many big idea questions are explored:

- What do they need to create a society?
- How might they work together?
- What kind of character will become normal in your society?

Students are split into groups of 4 per group and given a bag of necessary supplies. In the bag they'll find exactly what they will need to build a structure, create rules and norms for their society. They'll be asked to communicate cohesively in the 30 minute time limit and construct a structure with landscaping around it; all while creating rules and norms for their society. Each person in the group has a job to support the greater good. There are consequence cards to throw unexpected challenges at them, if they are not working together. The "queen" (me) will come and intentionally take one of their supplies from them as a punishment to see how they respond. Infusing chaos and uncertainty into their ecosystem pushes them to become both united as a team and flexible learners capable of adapting to the world around them.

When they are demonstrating powerful character and cooperation, they are gifted additional supplies. As a teacher, I'm basically completely off limits during this project. They have to try and resolve all of their problems, questions, and conflicts during the simulation entirely on their own. I love using this activity as a culminating activity after we have done intentional character work with smaller project based learning assignments. The success or failure of this project really helps me uncover if they are ready for more and can move to the next level with their learning.

 **<u>Self-Reflection:</u>**

Do you intentionally teach students what character looks like before, during, and after PBL?

Do you exclude students from group work because it's easier for you or classmates, and/or they simply request to work alone?

How do you know your students all understand what character looks like during group work or project based learning?

How might you intentionally teach character during your next experiential learning project?

What life lesson informed your perspective on experiential learning?

Share out your reflections using #InspiringJ🍎Y

AFFIRMATIONS

(Write, Draw, or Brainstorm ideas or thoughts here)

I AM AN EXPERIENTIAL LEARNER BECAUSE...

Joyful leaders reflect from experiences of listening and learning. From the moment Jennifer brilliantly shares her guiding "LESSICONS", she navigates readers with a strategic framework to effectively understand how to increase student engagement with purposeful thinking. The journey she communicates challenges us to thoughtfully identify practical steps to be curious alongside our students. Building authentic relationships is the key to creating a healthy school culture that will increase trust and opportunities for accountable learning. Intentional inspiration of JOY is a discipline we can promote and grow into with heart.

Jillian DuBois, Elementary Educator, Author + Illustrator

LESSON 9:

WAKE-UP CALL - REMINDERS

 **Launch:**

When I was in my second year teaching I remember sitting in a meeting with a parent of an honors student. At the time, I was teaching math to this student who was struggling in my class. The student was not doing their work and had lots of academic and behavioral problems outside of my classroom they were dealing with. Unfortunately, the parent really started attacking me and telling me I was a bad teacher and I wasn't doing anything correctly with their child. Basically, they believed it was my responsibility to hold their child's hand and do everything for them. I remember thinking that perhaps the learner should be put in one of my on grade level classes instead. At the time, I held honors students to a higher standard. I know this is wrong now, but back then, I was convinced that I was doing what's right.

On top of it, my principal was highly critical in the meeting about how I collected papers and instructed me to start individually collecting them from each student. As a middle school math teacher, I relied on my turn-in basket, like most every teacher in our building. Typically, when we were done correcting an assignment students put their papers in the basket. Later, I'd go and grab the pile and put them in the gradebook. This process seemed simple enough and generally worked for most students. Being new to teaching, I followed the same classroom procedures as the other teachers in my building. They had way more experience than me...

Who was I to question all of these veteran teachers' procedures?

My principal openly criticized me in front of an already frustrated parent, essentially calling me out, and detailing how my turn-in process was a bad idea. It was a HUGE WAKE-UP CALL! Needless to say, I was initially pissed off, embarrassed, and hurt. When you are made to feel stupid and small in front of someone, it's almost impossible to feel supported, as anger and hurt feelings surround the situation. While low character rants will often temporarily change behavior, many times, relationships are unimaginably damaged. In truth, I never trusted that principal or felt connected to them again. However, after coming home and taking a thoughtful pause, I was able to calm down and gain a deeper level of perspective on my actual class procedure. This pause, known as "Emotional Granularity" (David, 2016) is when we label our emotions to help us pinpoint the cause and experience of what we're feeling. This is why veteran teachers always suggest sitting on an upsetting parent email overnight before responding. The time helps us create a "linguistic separation to tease out a productive path moving forward."

What did I really think about what the principal was saying?

Did she tell me at the right time and in the right manner? NO.

Did she demonstrate respect for me while she berated me? NO.

But, and here's the really important question: was she right about my failed turn-in procedure? Well...YES.

I literally changed my policy overnight and it is one of the best decisions I've ever made. When we have paper assignments that need to be collected, I now walk around to the entire class and collect them myself.

And during COVID-19, when our schools shut down, teachers did the same thing but virtually, checking in with every student either over Zoom or through a messaging system. This brief individual connection allows us to verify they put their name on the assignment, ensure they have it all completed and personally check for understanding.

It's an amazing opportunity to uncover possible questions or barriers to student learning. Learners are able to communicate how they are doing with their assignment and what support they need from me to get their work finished successfully. Powerful student check-ins act as a reminder for me to establish a high level of trust, seek feedback about student progress, and what changes are necessary to support students' needs. These daily reminders of student learning aide teachers to reflect on our lessons through the lens of our learners.

Additionally, when giving students feedback I always lean into positivity. Some of our best lessons come from learning what not to do. While my principal helped me see an overdue change in my class structure, she also inadvertently modeled a poor way to maintain relationships with the people we lead.

> Positive reminders help students and teachers partner toward building an Award Winning Culture in the classroom.

Reminders are important!.

 Expectations: Students will learn to demonstrate academic character through intentional character modeling.

 Stuff: Clear and consistent set of reminders and routine.

 Skills: By intentionally modeling character, students will learn to be self-aware and become responsible decision makers while working on relationship skills and self-management.

Instruction/Activities:

Each day, my students walk into our room, they are warmly greeted by me at the door while the screen lists out all of the supplies they will need for the day. The daily visual reminder includes necessary materials, first steps, and a JOY Launcher for the day. Leading with character means we can discuss concepts at the start of the day. Students complete the task and then we discuss the meaning and how it connects to today's purpose. Pairing our daily work with character inspiration helps crystalize a growth mindset ready to persevere through the day's challenges. In essence, it energizes student mindfulness to attack our lesson by doing the right thing!

Learners are also prepared by having all of their materials out and ready; thus, eliminating surprises that will cause anxiety. [Will I need my coloring supplies, workbook, or red pen?] When teachers fail to post expectations, students become preoccupied with trips to their locker, problem-solving concerns over supplies, and other non-essential to learning type barriers.

Using positivity to reinforce desired behavior happens with educational POWER. Teachers must always practice POSITIVITY ON WORK, EVALUATIONS, and REMINDERS.

POWER

Positivity

On

Work

Evaluations

Reminders

When we are teaching students to behave with high character and essentially reminding them to do the right thing—we as teachers also have to be driven to do the right thing! Reflecting on one's own character is an outstanding way to inspire our students' moral compass. Sometimes, I am just as guilty as other adults who default to raising my voice, in order to get a student to stop an action. Wouldn't treating learners with respect and dignity be a stronger approach?

One big problem at our school: HATS!!

Students are not permitted to wear hats at school and are constantly forgetting to take them off upon entering the building each morning. Simply yelling, "TAKE YOUR HAT OFF" might change the current behavior but has no reasonable chance of reminding students of the bigger character takeaways. Instead, I use a more empathic approach and say, "Good morning, would you mind taking your hat off for me?" Ironically, treating students with respect and assuming best intentions repeatedly earn me a smile, removal of said hat, and a stronger student relationship.

WILL YOU DO THE RIGHT THING?

I love wearing hats myself on the weekends and sometimes I completely forget I have it on. Aren't students capable of forgetting as well? Empathy empowers me to understand the feeling of wearing the hat to school, simply forgetting it's even on and walking into the building to go to class. This is something that can be solved easily with a little positive energy and respect.

Another hot topic at our school is cell phones. Anyone who teaches middle or high school has experienced the challenge of incorporating these technological distractions. I believe in an effective way to introduce this into my classrooms...

WE MUST TEACH STUDENTS HOW, WHEN, AND WHY TO USE THEIR PHONES.

Our class policy is that it's acceptable to use one's phone as long as we are both showing respect and using it for educational purposes. However, when you have free time, you are welcome to check messages, reminders or fun things on your phone. On the flip side, I also understand that some teachers are not ready to allow phones yet in their classrooms; but leading with high character reminders are still important. Please don't post giant signs with a cell phone and a slash through it. Visual reminders that steer entirely toward compliance, management, and power erode relationships. You can share this expectation in a positive tone. Teachers can hang a sign that has all of the following options: phones in use today, phones put away until we need them, or phones will be out of sight for today's lesson. Here is an example poster you could have in your room.

Example cell phone use poster.

You can explain that there are options and each day you will have the arrow on a different set of instructions. But if you're going to be comfortable in hanging that sign of phone possible options; please, have the wherewithal to follow your own class expectations, regarding YOUR own phone use.

 ## Close Intentionally:

Another great reminder is to take some time out of each week to spotlight character in other classes, besides just advisory, or during weekly meetings. You can have the students listen to a podcast on character, read an article or story about it, and focus on something that is related to your subject area.

Remember to also always give shout outs to students that are showing amazing character. These shoutouts can be in the moment, or you could recognize a student once a week who showed amazing character for what they are doing in your class. Focusing on character rather than academic content might feel like a departure from core instruction. However, it's the exact type of lesson planning that builds greater meaning into what your students are currently learning. Keeping character front and center reminds everyone what YOU, as the teacher, values: grit, hard work, growth mindset, integrity, and risk-taking.

 ## Opportunities:

When I taught elementary school, I wrote out the schedule for the entire day on the board with two columns: on one side was the activity and the other was the supplies or materials students would need for that activity. For instance, when students returned from recess or transitioned from one activity to another, they instantly knew exactly what they would need to grab to be successful.

At all levels, I've started everyday with a morning meeting with an emphasis on character. Whether it's a question, involves reading a children's book, short story, or poem, we'd discuss what we needed out of the day and how it would look for everyone involved. An example discussion might be: how might we work together during our group project today? What will a successful group sound, feel or look like? When students generate specific actionable words for a lesson's expectations they're more likely to find success.

 ## Needs:

You know that you have created essential reminders when you have a sub in your classroom and come back to a note which shares how your students explained the routines and how the classroom functioned. Showing great respect to a substitute and continuing on with positive classroom norms, procedures, and systems indicates that students are soaking up your character reminders.

 **Self-Reflection:**

How are you welcoming students into your room?

Are you informing them of what to expect for the day?

How are you correcting students? Is it always positive, or do you let negativity creep into your work?

Are you focusing on character even when it takes time away from your curriculum?

What's a personal lesson from your own life that reminds you to focus on character?

Share out your reflections using #InspiringJOY

AFFIRMATIONS

(Write, Draw, or Brainstorm ideas or thoughts here)

The reminder I want my learners to leave with is...

Inspiring JOY is more than a book; it's also a tool and resource for every educator! The way Jennifer Appel creates synergy between personal stories, lesson plan ideas, and SEL knowledge is truly **CAPTIVATING** and will leave you feeling passionate and excited about creating a movement of **JOY** and autonomy in your classroom with your students! This is one book that every educator will learn and gain insight from, regardless of the content or grade level you teach!
Lindsay Titus, K-12 Behavior Specialist, Mindset and Behavior Coach with DEFINE YOUniversity

Character Lesson Plan

Character -- Will you do the right thing?

 LAUNCH:

Can someone give me a definition of character? (Character is moral or mental qualities distinctive to an individual.) What might outstanding character look like? Does anyone know what it means to do the right thing?

EXPECTATIONS:

- Teacher Note: Focusing on skills such as sharing and compromising under an umbrella of generosity, primes the learning pump for bigger soft skills like kindness and empathy.
- Students will be able to distribute a diverse set of items in an equitable (not necessarily equal) manner.
- Students will do the right thing by gathering input from all members.
- Students will learn how to collectively make inclusive informed decisions.
- Students will learn the definition of character and what it means to do the right thing.

 STUFF:

- Cups filled with incentives your students will enjoy (candy, token economy pieces, pencils, stickers, etc.). Teachers will seek input from a diverse group of students to ensure a culturally responsive list of incentives.
- Groups of 3-4 students (you can choose or let them).
- Fill the cups with an odd number of treats, if you have 3 in a group then have 5 items in the cup, make sure they can't divide them evenly.
- Also, make sure each group has a different amount. Maybe a group of 3 gets 4 items, and one gets 7 items, etc.

SKILLS:

Students will learn all 5 CASEL skills: Social-Awareness, Self-Management, Social Awareness, Relationship Skills, and Responsible Decision Making.

INSTRUCTION/ACTIVITES:

- Teacher Note: Don't give students any hints as to how you want them to make decisions, let this be an organic process.
  - You will hand out the cups to each group and the goal is to have them use a decision making process to decide how to distribute the items fairly.
- Tell them you are going to hand out these cool cups to each group, but first we need to set some rules.
- Rule #1: You are not allowed to touch the cup until I have handed them out to every group.

85

- Rule #2: You are not allowed to raise your voice or use any name calling.
- Rule #3: You decide as a collective group how all of the items are distributed amongst your group.
- Rule #4: You don't have to take all of the items in the cup, you can leave some in the cup.
- Rule #5: Everyone in the group must be satisfied with the outcome at the end.
- Pass out the cups to each group, make sure it is in a central location for all group members to see.
- Once you have passed out all of the cups, tell them they can dump out the contents and start their distribution process, give them about 3-5 minutes to do this.
- While they are making decisions as a group, walk around and observe how they are deciding, see if a leader emerges in the group, are they just talking or are they using a method like rock, paper, scissors to decide? Make notes so that you can include this in the discussion.
- When all of the items have been distributed and the groups all agree and are happy with the decisions, stop them.

 ## CLOSE INTENTIONALLY:

- Ask the group as a whole, is everyone satisfied with what you got from the cup. If someone is not happy, ask them why, what happened in the group to cause this?
    - Groups that are happy with all of the decisions, how did you decide who got what? (you will see kids doing rock, paper, scissors, or discussing what they need or like in the cup and then giving those items away)
    - Was there a leader that emerged at your group? Was this helpful? Why? (You will have students that took control and it may have helped speed up the process and helped to ask questions to see what all the likes/dislikes are in the group).
    - Did any group leave items in the cup? Why? (You will hear that maybe they couldn't decide who to give them to, so it was only fair that no one got them).
    - How does this relate to our question, "Will you do the Right Thing?" How did you do the right thing in your group?
    - What does this say about our character?
    - How did cultural differences impact your decision making? (Maybe you have a student with specific dietary needs, maybe for religious purposes they were only able to choose certain items, maybe their race or identity impacted an element of the process).

 ## OPPORTUNITIES:

- For elementary school, have an equal amount of items but still choose different items for them to share. This may need to have a little more direction at the beginning, giving them a few strategies to help decide who will get each item.
- For high school you may want to have items that appeal to them, like homework passes, getting out of class 5 minutes early, food, etc..

 ## NEEDS:

- Throughout the year, I randomly give out snacks to my class during an activity. It may be popcorn, crackers, pretzels, candy, etc. I set a plate in the middle of a table group and they would be expected to share the snacks. I wouldn't divide them up into individual portions, I would just have them share. This is a great way to assess their progress and see if they need work in any areas. You will see the groups that all stare at the plate and are afraid to touch the food, some that wait until the whole class has some and ask permission to start eating, others that devour the entire plate and forget about others in the group. You can really see how you are progressing as a class and you know you are at a good point in learning when everyone can share the snacks respectfully and express to their group members what they need and want.

- After COVID-19, this snack lesson takes the form of individual snack bags, like crackers, pretzels, cookies. Give a variety for students to choose from in a group.
- Family Connection: One of the ways to continue the work of building character is to involve families in the process. 81% of parents believe that SEL & Character are just as important as academic learning (McGraw-Hill Education, 2018). Here is an example post that you could print and send home with kids, post on social media and your learning management system, or send in an email.

CHARACTER

Character is moral or mental qualities distinctive to an individual.

WILL YOU DO THE RIGHT THING?

In class today, we did an activity to help us learn about decision making and doing the right thing for others and ourselves.

Here are some reflection questions for you to discuss as a family:

- What are some ways that you feel you do the right thing?
- How do you make decisions so that everyone feels valued?
- What does high character look like in your family?

 SELF-REFLECTION:

- Reflect about your class:
  - Who is showing leadership? (They need to be given responsibility to influence a group or activity)
  - Who had a hard time and couldn't express their feelings/ideas well? (They need to be given a way to communicate with you that is not public, like email, social media, Google Classroom).
  - As a whole, did they learn about their own character and have the skills to make decisions? If not, intentionally teaching some decision making skills (rock, paper, scissors, learning to listen to others opinions, voting, etc.).

UNIT 2: EXCELLENCE

While all educators strive for excellence in and out of the classroom, teaching learners to do their very best is a profound gift that gives all schools an advantage to set up students for life success. In *Award Winning Culture*, Appel boils down the four E's of Excellence: Engagement, Empowerment, Experiential, and E.P.I.C.. He inspires readers to relook at autonomy and influence to reach for new heights of engagement. By mobilizing students and staff for good, educational leaders can bring out the best in all stakeholders. Additionally, voice and choice become paramount to ongoing empowerment opportunities. While experiential learning has long been a wonderful hands-on classroom technique, in a school-wide framework, leaders have a chance to have an awesome reach by building in relevance, purpose, and authentic audience to all efforts with school culture and climate. Appel's E.P.I.C model helps educators pick apart and energize a host of school wide programs, processes, events, and procedures.

While these big picture ideas have a wonderful positive impact on a global school-wide system; perhaps, the classroom is the most beautiful canvas to bring student-agency to life. Armed with a pedagogical understanding, teachers become the school culture masterminds to effect lasting change with every learner. Pay particular attention to the LESSICONS in this section as they provide a best practice model for reaching our most at-risk students.

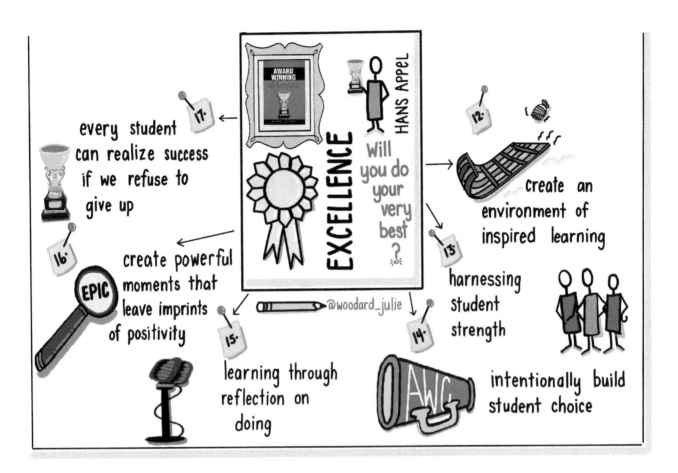

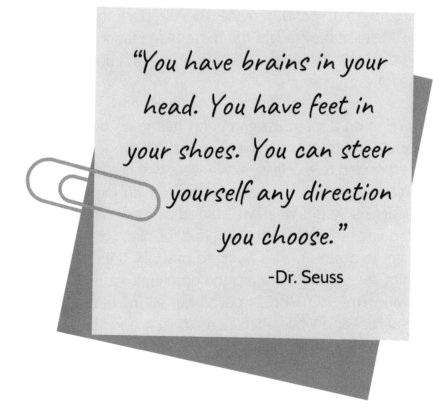

"You have brains in your head. You have feet in your shoes. You can steer yourself any direction you choose."

-Dr. Seuss

LESSON 10:

MOONING - ENGAGEMENT

🚀 Launch:

During one of my first years in teaching, I taught in a program called Focus. Focus was an alternative type classroom filled with students who struggled with behavior. Some students had ties to gangs, other students had frequented juvenile detention; meanwhile, a couple learners wore full time ankle monitors. It was a hardcore room of young adolescents who had been forced to grow up far too quickly. As you'd imagine, they were often in trouble not only at school but outside of school as well. They had some difficult life situations that created real barriers for them to function in a traditional school setting. Things like poverty, mental health, and a history of abuse were generally present among these high ACEs (adverse childhood experiences) learners. They had been placed into this self contained classroom to try and provide the support that they needed to be successful. Some days I felt like they taught me more than I taught them. I remember one student who taught me an incredible lesson about engaging education and how it didn't need to look the same for everyone.

One day we were working on a math assignment. I had gone over the information in a very traditional manner and then they were asked to work independently on the assignment that corresponded to the lesson. We were working on fractions—everyone's favorite (cue the sarcasm)! He was perfectly respectful during the lesson and didn't interrupt or fight back against it. But when we started doing the independent practice he showed no interest in doing the worksheet that I had for him. I tried bargaining with him. [If you did this...you'll get to do this.] I was trying to basically bribe him into compliance. I tried reasoning with him and helping him with the problems. I attempted to see if I could work out a problem with him—NOTHING! I pulled out all my best classroom strategies: wait time, proximity, space. For a while, I left him alone and focused on other students, before eventually coming back around to him.

In my own head, I was doing my job and he was just being difficult at this point. When I finally chose to come back around to him, I was clearly frustrated and said *'can you please just do a few problems.'* What followed next was a dreadful ultimatum: *'if you don't, you will have to stay after class and finish.'*

Any predictions on how this vail threat went over on my young oppositional learner?

He just looked straight at me, and started swearing. He was spitting words at me that I didn't even know existed. [I actually had to ask my husband about a few later, because I had never heard them before]. He then said, F*** YOU, B**** and ran out of the room.

Because we were in a portable that was at the edge of campus, and it was the last class of the day, he chose to run straight out to the bus pick up. Obviously, I wanted to make sure he was safe; so, I escorted the rest of my students to the bus and lingered around to make sure everyone was on. I knew that I could 'deal' with my angry student on his return the next day. Ideally, he could cool off that night and be back tomorrow to figure out what was happening. While I started waving to the students as they pulled away from campus, my overwhelmed learner stuck his head out the window and said,

"This is what I think of you, Mrs. Appel" as he turned around and MOONED me.

Ever been mooned by a student?

I have to admit now, it was a truly humiliating experience, having a student scream, yell profanities, and then moon me for all my other students to witness. Staying calm, grounded, and patient in that moment was excruciatingly challenging. Needless to say, I was pissed that night and I came home frustrated with all my negative energy focused on completely the wrong person. I had placed all of the blame on my student by focusing on what he had done. Was it wrong? YES! It's hard to reach cultural excellence in a classroom when a student throws an all out fit. But, did I have a part in what happened? ABSOLUTELY! Unfortunately, he was suspended for a few days, which is not the best solution, but it gave me a chance to reflect. I needed to gather my thoughts and figure out how to be better. I needed to reset my mind about this student and realize that he wasn't the enemy. The time helped me to re-examine a trauma informed lens to best understand and partner with this student. Additionally, I needed to make a big change to create a classroom with more relevance to support his needs while fostering his passions.

Thanks to John Hattie's research we know that the teacher to student relationship is greatly impactful to student learning outcomes. But new research from Dr. Clayton Cook, et all, has re-explored the way in which we view relationships. According to Cook, relationships are in a forever continuum between establishing, maintaining, and restoring (repairing) them. [*Using the EMR method of relationship cultivation, the researchers found a 33% increase in academic performance and a 75% decrease in disruptive behavior*].

In other words, a relationship is never stagnant as we find ourselves in a perpetual state of flux. Teachers who find the greatest learning outcomes that Hattie reinforces use a tracking system to better identify where they are on the continuum with each student.

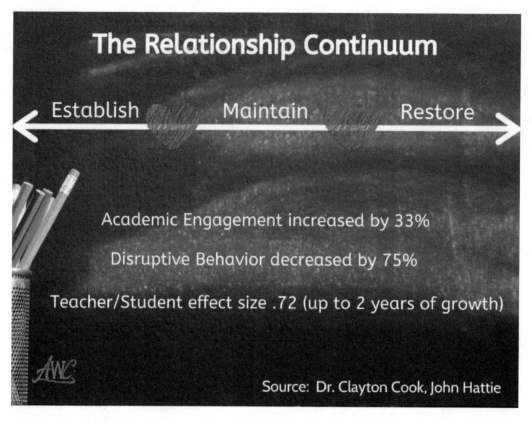

It doesn't take a PHD to realize I was in desperate need of repairing and restoring my relationship with my mooning buddy. This was the time for me to model my highest example of character (humility, patience, and empathy).

INSPIRING JOY IS ABOUT SHOWING UP TO DIFFICULT EMOTIONS WITH COMPASSION AND CURIOSITY, RATHER THAN FEAR AND JUDGEMENT.

Upon his return, I smiled at him, apologized, and genuinely welcomed him back to my room. Repairing our relationship became a focal point in my world. When he walked in, his head was down. He didn't even want to look me in the eye as he was clearly ashamed of what had happened. I was very kind to him and shared how I cared about him and would actively make school more meaningful for him. I also reiterated that I didn't judge him because of his actions. I assured him we could start over and have a re-do to form a stronger relationship. Welcoming him back with grace, took experienced amounts of patience.

> *"Patience is bitter, but its fruit is sweet."*
> *-Aristotle*

He looked at me like I was crazy as trusting an adult was not a normal part of his world...but eventually he came around and understood that I wasn't leaving and how much I cared about him. He was extremely successful that year and we worked to make meaning in his education by helping him understand what he was working toward with goal setting, reflection, and a strengths based approach. To be honest, I now look at his outlandish behavior as a gift. His over the top reaction to my compliance focused instruction opened my eyes and eventually helped me transform into a much better teacher by closing the vulnerability loop in our relationship.

Now, the great part is that I saw him years later at his work, all grown up and self-regulated. His heartfelt smile and thank-you meant the world to me. He went on to tell me that I was a huge influence in his life and he still couldn't believe that I forgave him for what he did. [It's incredible what grace, repair, and assuming best intentions can do for a relationship.] He was the first in his family to graduate from high school. He has maintained a steady job, stayed out of trouble and has the self confidence to see a bright future for himself. Just writing about him now fills me with such a deep sense of pride for the young man he's become.

It's ironic that the real exposure that day wasn't of his behind...but instead of the fact that I wasn't serving all my students. Looking back now, I believe this failure was all on me. I was giving an inordinately boring lesson that had no purpose in his current life and then trying to force him to do a stupid worksheet that he wouldn't remember later.

AUTHORITY TOWARD FORCED COMPLIANCE, COUPLED WITH POOR LESSON PLANNING IS A RECIPE FOR DISASTER.

Teachers must build in autonomy and influence to ensure engaging lessons within the classroom. The truth is, if educators don't provide opportunities to discover and develop real purpose, some students will find undesirable ways of communicating our shortcomings.

We must foster autonomy and influence in our classes, otherwise our students will call us out on it, quietly checkout, or fail to reach their highest potential.

 Expectations: When you teach a subject, stop focusing on getting through all of the content. Slow down and think about what are the essentials and teach them to the fullest extent with engagement for students.

 Stuff: Engaging lessons!

 Skills: Relationship skills are key to creating engaging lessons for students. You have to create a relationship with each student, and they in turn create those relationships with each other.

 Instruction/Activities:

Great leaders in the work of engagement like Dave Burgess, Teach Like a Pirate, are amazing at inspiring students. I remember seeing him do his keynote presentation and I couldn't stop looking at him and just hung on his every word. This is the type of involvement we all want in our classrooms. We want our students to LOVE coming to our classes, and we want them to feel empowered to learn and create.

I think that one of my biggest mistakes early in my career was that I was so concerned with standards and making sure that we covered everything that needed to get done. It really didn't matter if they mastered it, I just needed to get through the information. If they missed something they could catch up later when it was reviewed the next year. This was such a huge mistake. I was being a compliant teacher and just doing what I was told instead of what was best for my students. With the age of technology and students having cell phones that are set up like slot machines constantly buzzing and giving them instant stimulation, they are not going to sit and listen to a lecture and then do a worksheet. A few students may because they are compliant and they will get an A in your class. They follow the rules and take notes, do the worksheet and pass the test because they are good at memorizing information. But the question remains even for our most compliant learners: did they actually learn anything?

We must ensure each student is engaged in the lesson in order for them to want to learn. While traditional education is a system to reward student compliance through grades, credits, and diplomas--Learning is a voluntary endeavor to promote purposeful growth.

WHAT IF SCHOOL TRANSFORMED INTO AN EDUCATION SYSTEM TO REWARD EMPOWERED THINKING WITH JOYOUS LEARNING?

With the mooning student, I realized that I couldn't just teach math in the traditional sense. I had to make the lessons engaging and something that was relevant to them. One of the concepts that I was teaching was fractions and percentages; so, we set up a simulation store and they had to calculate totals with tax and discounts. They were given money and they had to use that money for the month to live off of. They had to pay rent, utilities, car payments, food, everything to live. They had to pay to live the life that they dreamed of.

Learners also had to earn money so they were paid for doing certain "jobs" around the classroom and in other subjects. Students could also work overtime to earn extra money, and even work on holidays and they would get paid time and a half. It was such a fun project for them to see how math related to their life. They had to really apply all of their skills to this world that they would eventually be living in and see what it took to survive with the money earned.

One of my students even decided to open an investment firm and he would invest your money for you in the stocks and calculate the percentage based on the actual stock market and give payouts, only after he took a percentage of course. But he was learning more sophisticated math than if I had done a lecture and taught him about how to convert a percent to a decimal.

Engaging REAL life simulations have learning applications outside of school.

 ### Close Intentionally:

I am giving you permission to relook at your standards. What's most important? Is there a way to combine concepts to create an engaging unit to teach many different concepts at once? Can you cut back on some of the drill and kill and try to find ways to make your lessons more exciting?

This close look at our standards really built momentum at the beginning of Covid-19. We were forced to spend less time with students; therefore, giving us an opportunity to evaluate our standards and break them down to their core seeking the most salient content. If we focus on students truly engaging in the times we see them, learners will remember concepts far into the future rather than only during our classes. The goal of learning is not to pass my class. The goal of learning is to ensure my students can apply their work when my class is but a distant memory.

> *"Our job as teachers is not to prepare kids for something; our job is to help kids learn to prepare themselves for anything."*
> *-A.J. Juliani*

 ## Opportunities:

For elementary level, I highly recommend reading Kristen Nan and Jacie Maslyk's book, *All In: Taking a Gamble in Education*. As an elementary teacher Nan does amazing work with engagement in her classroom. Her students are learning so many practical skills to use later. Practicality is critical at all ages and Nan's creativity is a model for all teachers.

Engagement is about thinking creatively when designing learning opportunities. And as Jason Sudeikis says "creativity is making the invisible...visible." There's an unexplainable electricity that teachers experience when their creative flow results in powerful student learning. Here's a couple tips for maximizing creativity:

- Use speech to text dictation on your phone to record notes when inspiration strikes
- Take a walk
- Listen to music
- Participate in a free association brain dump with a member of your PLN or PLC
- Keep a small notepad at your bedside to jot down a quick idea
- Begin each day with a 10 minute nonsensical free write with no restrictions.
- Read, Watch, or listen to inspiring non-educators
- Put the phone away while venturing out to a museum, live theater show, or culture rich dining experience.

Creativity is a muscle that you must exercise and can be even more powerful when brainstorming with others. Psychologists call this rapid fire sharing of creative ideas, **burstiness** and it's filled with energy and intensity. The most important element is to get out of your comfort zone and give your fresh creative lesson idea a try. It does students no good if you keep your award winning instruction sitting in a forever locked planning book. Try. Fail. Reflect. Modify. TRY AGAIN.

> *"Teachers who act like scientists are much more likely to find classroom success because they view each lesson as an opportunity to test their theory of learning, by staying curious while listening to the experience of their students."*
> *-Hans Appel*

 **Needs:**

You know that you are engaging students when they want nothing more than to come to your class. Or in my case they all said math was their favorite subject and they begged me to move on to the next grade level math class....what? When you have students that find real purpose and engagement in their work they will continue to grow and use these skills in other areas of their life.

 **Self-Reflection:**

Do you have students in your classes that are getting good grades and listening but are NOT truly engaging?

Can they take the knowledge they are learning in your class and apply it outside of your environment?

Think of a life lesson that a student taught you. How has it shaped your engagement practices?

Share out your reflections using #InspiringJOY

AFFIRMATIONS

(Write, Draw, or Brainstorm ideas or thoughts here)

I AM AN ENGAGING TEACHER BECAUSE...

Jennifer's transparency about her successes and challenges are a **REFRESHING** take for developing teacher leaders. She provides a variety of practical strategies educators can use to create joyful learning experiences for students of all ages.
P. Sloan Joseph, Equity Advocate & Instructional Coach-Greater is in Me, LLC

LESSON 11:

DYSLEXIA - EMPOWERMENT

 ## Launch:

"You just CAN'T read...can you? You're not even trying."

When I was in 2nd grade, my teacher started noticing that I had difficulty reading. Despite LOVING books and the practice of reading it was a little harder for me than the other kids. I had nightmares of my teacher showing increasing frustration for my inability to pass basic reading tests.

To understand the complexity of my situation, you must recall that I come from a long line of educators (teachers, principals, para-professionals, and superintendents). Indeed, I was set up with EVERY possible familia advantage to succeed with my schooling. And ironically, my elementary school principal was my own father. After mustering up the courage to present her concerns to my dad about my reading deficits, my teacher recommended I be tested for special education. After some discussion, the school team agreed to give me a full evaluation (IQ, achievement, etc.).

Unbenounced to me, the results were quite compelling. Apparently, I did remarkably well on the IQ portion of the test. [More on that later...]

Needless to say, after uncovering such a surprising result, the school team started pushing my family to completely switch gears and explore gifted testing. I can only imagine this 180 degree educational change of direction must have thrown my school support team for quite a loop. After acing the math portion of the gifted entrance exams, I again struggled on the reading portion (similar to my class performance). Because my father was the building principal, he could have easily used his power and influence to override gifted policy to bump me into advanced classes. My family decided to pause and weigh their options. Because I was still struggling in reading performance, 'we' elected NOT to place me in the gifted program.

Here's the most noteworthy part, I wasn't told about any of the results and ultimately knew nothing about my documented intelligence. The evaluations, IQ tests, and implications were put into a dusty keepsake box with pictures and other memories, not to be discovered for the next 12 years.

Throughout the remainder of elementary and into middle and high school, I found solid success. I was an exceptionally compliant, gritty, hard working student who earned outstanding grades and buried whatever learning insecurities deep down. Although I always managed to earn A's, from time to time, I really struggled on certain tests. Luckily with retakes, extra credit and homework...I managed to keep my grades at an exceptional level. As you might expect, I knew from when I was a little girl that I wanted to be a teacher. Nothing would stop my pursuit of a lifelong dream to work with kids.

However, during my sophomore year of college, I hit my first major roadblock in my quest to reach the education program. After failing a basic reading entrance exam, the waves of insecurities came rushing back. Truthfully, in my darkest moments, I seriously contemplated quitting school; as I questioned my ability to pass a fairly basic assessment. After looking closely at my grades, educational history, and my current failing entrance test...an administrator at CWU's ed program suggested that I might consider being tested for dyslexia. The results won't surprise you.

After a battery of exploration, I was diagnosed with dyslexia and presented with overdue information on strategies to overcome this learning hurdle. Armed with a better understanding of myself and some tools to maximize my brain's strengths, I eventually aced the exam and got into the ed program.

One weekend, during these college days my eventual husband and I found ourselves back at home visiting with my parents about the enlightening test results. Our conversation coincided with my mom's sudden appearance with a box of pictures for me to take back to college. As we dug through the old box filled with awkward funny pictures and laughed at how my parents dressed me in the 80's, a couple documents caught my attention. As I pulled them out, and began looking over these tattered official looking "evaluation results," I wasn't immediately sure of what I was looking at. I handed the stack of memorabilia over to Hans to see if he could make sense of what I was seeing.

[*In Hans's preparation to become a school counselor, he was taking courses in statistics, assessment, and evaluation. Studying and administering IQ tests gave him insight into what he was seeing in this dusty old folder.*]

Until that moment, I had never seen or heard of these IQ results. As we started to dig through assessment research; and more specifically how exceptional my results truly were; this complicated brain puzzle finally started to fit together.

Let's just say, I blew the IQ test out of the water! My overall IQ was rated at 156. For those not very familiar with IQ testing here's a quick reference guide:

90-110	AVERAGE
110-120	HIGH AVERAGE
120-130	SUPERIOR
130+	VERY SUPERIOR/ EXTREMELY HIGH

Mensa, the world's international high IQ society requires a 132 for membership. For my mathematically inclined readers my IQ was multiple standard deviations outside the norm. 156 is in the top 1% in the country. [For comparison, Albert Einstein was estimated to be at approximately 160]. My IQ coupled with other reading challenges matched extensive bodies of research that suggests dyslexia is often accompanied by high IQ. It finally made some sense. For years, I had explained to teachers how my brain would essentially take a snapshot of textbook images that I eventually learned was called a photographic memory. Oddly, I've always had the gift and curse of being able to take mental images of a page from a book and later recall the smallest of details from the page. Being liberated to understand my own brain freed me up to imagine a world where I was smart.

> *"Everyone is a genius, but if you judge a fish by its ability to climb a tree, it will spend its whole life believing it is stupid."*
> -Albert Einstein

After eventually getting into the ed program, I went on to earn a degree as a reading specialist. Fast forward several years later, I earned a Masters in Literacy and was in the early stages of a successful career in education. The irony that I'm writing this text (my third book) after a 20+ year career in education filled with awards and recognitions is not lost on me. If I'm being honest, I'm both proud and a little taken back by some of the literary praise I've accomplished.

No surprise to anyone, my own struggles continue to arm me with a special empathy for students, who have a hard road in school. And I believe that having both a gifted mind coupled with a learning disability gives me a unique educational advantage in working with a range of student issues. I look at my struggles with NO bitterness, sadness or wistful imagery. Indeed, I believe these hurdles made me into who I was meant to be, in a way that Jim Collins, best-selling author of Good To Great reinforces there are "things we are wired to do." My innate superpower or 'wiring' has helped me specialize with struggling learners.

But I can't help but wonder how this story would have gone with less educationally focused parents and a child without my resilient and single minded determination to become a future teacher.

I recently heard Jimmy Casas preach about the need to play to our student's strengths and stop focusing on compliance. This hit me in such a profound and personal way because I often wonder how my own educational experience might have looked different under alternative circumstances.

How many kids wouldn't have been COMMITTED to do extra credit, retake tests or ask lots of questions in class? How many children lack the strategies to OVERCOME their deficits? How many students give up before they've IDENTIFIED their career JOY? How many college kids DROP OUT, when their desired outcome gets fuzzy? How many children don't truly understand how their OWN brains are wired?

I survived almost 14 years of education before someone solved my learning puzzle. And while all of this may have made me who I am today, it scares the heck out of me...

Which students are we missing? Are we willing to share evaluation results with students? Which current culturally biased systems prevent us from playing to our students' strengths? Do our struggling students ACTUALLY believe they are smart? Are our educational practices fostering an inherent belief in children? Who's job is it to instill HOPE by empowering our learners?

It took me years before I had tangible proof that I was smart, when in reality we are ALL smart. And to be honest, it took a few more years after that weekend moment digging through pictures and evaluation reports before I actually believed it. On a hard day, I still question myself at times when I think of things in a different way than everyone else, reverting back to the occasional negative self talk questioning my intelligence.

> Teachers who inspire JOY foster student resilencency, grit, and passion for learning, through a deliberate focus on student strengths by empowering them to have voice and choice in their learning.

There are students in your office, classroom, or school RIGHT NOW, who are ABSOLUTELY CONVINCED that they can't, won't or never will. Will you simply assume that they have the parents, internal drive, and vision to discover their passion on their own.

OR...will you help them discover their own genius?

Empowerment through student voice and choice.

 Expectations: Students will be able to work independently to accomplish the goal of learning.

 Stuff: Classrooms must move away from compliance and move towards learning.

 Skills: When we empower students, they are self-aware, socially aware, learn to self-manage, make responsible decisions, and work on relationship skills with classmates.

Instruction/Activities:

During the COVID-19 crisis, schools were out for an extended period of time. People were rushing to try and learn the newest technology to do distance learning. Zoom went from a 1 million dollar company to a 15 million dollar company in just a few weeks. The world was turned upside down and we were rushing to try and help everyone learn this new "normal".

One constant I noticed coming from all educational institutions were ways to help in the digital world with students to keep them compliant. Students were given rules to follow when they were in a Zoom classroom. They were given rules of when to do their homework. They were given schedules for what subjects to do each day. They were shown how to be compliant when they were not in the classroom. This made me think about what it must be like for all of these students when school is in session. Their life is all about compliance and how to follow the rules.

Does anyone else see a problem with this idea? Why are we so set on compliance instead of learning?

Now, after reading the above paragraph you might not be happy with me and may choose to stop reading or skip ahead. I think that there is a time and place for rules. We need to have rules in our society. But compliance only ensures we follow the rules under the watchful eyes of an authority figure: police, parent, boss, teacher, etc. On the other hand, empowerment inspires us to do our very best to create a civilized society regardless of who's observing us. We don't want a society that only follows the law when a police officer is present. Schools that only produce short-term memorization tied to classroom, school, and district mandates fail to propel life-long learning.

Law and order matter...but I also think that it shouldn't be our primary focus, we need to have rules and regulations, but we also need to focus on the most important parts of school; character, learning, creativity, joy, community, and purpose.

In my classroom I have flexible seating. When I say flexible seating, I am not just talking about cute comfortable furniture around my room. My classroom is full of choices in many different ways. By having flexible seating this helps students understand that they can learn in many different environments. Students learn through trial and error what works for them for a project. I remember having some students that really liked to have a desk and chair for when they were writing an essay and others that loved sitting in a comfy chair with a lapdesk for writing. Some students lay on the floor on a yoga mat and have a clipboard in front of them writing. They are able to choose for themselves what makes for the most successful writing environment for them.

Flexible Seating in my classroom.

[The funny thing is that I am currently typing this book on my laptop sitting on my bed with a lapdesk listening to Mozart.] I have students conference with me and discuss not only their academic work but also the environment they are working in. How do they feel about where they are sitting? Is it working? What would they change? By having the students reflect about their work environment and how productive they are, they are able to understand what it looks like for them to be successful, and it doesn't look the same for every person. My husband for example wrote his entire book standing at a standing desk in our office area, he would never use a lapdesk, he thinks they are extremely uncomfortable. We are both successful in our own right, but in very different environments.

Not only does this apply to your environment, this can also apply to reading specifically. As a person with dyslexia I don't do well with white paper and black writing, the stark contrast plays tricks with my brain. Thus, my Kindle is set to a green background when I read. When I have to look at a worksheet I do better with light blue, green, or pink as do most children. Guess what color I make copies in for my students? This is a small adjustment but worth the little time and effort it takes. With technology I tell my kids about my green Kindle screen so they can try it as well and they can see what works for them.

Earlier in Unit 1, I discussed the idea of extrinsic vs. intrinsic motivation and the fact that we want our students to be intrinsically motivated. This concept is huge in voice and choice. We want our students to get to the point that they are intrinsically motivated to learn and can create without a teacher around. This relates back to the compliance aspect. Teachers can't have students that are intrinsically motivated when all they are taught to be is compliant. If they are always doing what they are told, they are not able to explore on their own and learn what they are interested in.

> IN ORDER FOR STUDENTS TO TRULY BE MOTIVATED INTRINSICALLY THEY MUST RECEIVE AUTHENTIC CHOICE.

In my ELA class, they need to decide what they are going to read as a novel, how they are going to reflect while reading the book and then how they will express their learning at the end and present that to you. In PE, they need to be given the power to exercise in the manner that is best for them. I was an athlete growing up and loved to play volleyball, basketball, and many other sports. I can't stand softball nor am I good at it. I can't swing the bat, I am not good at catching a ball in the air, it doesn't matter how many times that I played in PE growing up it is not a skill that I possess. Why are we having students learning baseball and playing for weeks when it is not something that they will use in life to help with fitness? I wish I'd learned yoga growing up, as it is a life skill that I would have loved to explore. Why don't we have students come up with an exercise plan that they are going to accomplish during the year? Then, teachers can be available to help and train them in the ways that are best for them to accomplish their personal health goals. Students need to have more ownership over their learning, by encouraging students to ask for what they want to get out of a class.

 ## Close Intentionally:

When you are planning your next unit think about ways that you can have students infuse their own voice and choice. Are you willing to give them the power to decide what's best for their own learning?

 ## Opportunities:

Not all students are created the same. They're a mix of personality and character traits, experiences, cultural backgrounds, gender, age, and identity. Education can't be a one size fits all! You need to have your students choose the best ways to express their learning. This needs to be student driven and they need to decide what works best for them and how they can synthesize the information and express that to others and themselves.

Dena Simmons offers suggestions of how to become an anti-racist teacher through student empowerment and self discovery.

- Start with self - explore biases and self awareness
- Learn with your crew - connect with PLN, PLC, students, parents, community
- Affirm your students - instruction, interactions, curriculum must support ALL students
- Hold each other accountable
- Think about larger context - learn students' stories
- Ask students what they need

Dena Simmons, Edutopia, 2020

 ## Needs:

Testing should not always be the answer to having students show their knowledge. I don't know about you, but I passed a lot of tests in elementary, middle, and high school that I have no idea what they were about. I memorized the information so that I could pass and show compliance, but not actually learn anything. This happens a lot when we are only testing on facts and memorization. Students need to be showing their learning by synthesizing the information and applying it to their lives to really understand how the material connects to them and why it is important in the future.

 ## Self-Reflection:

Do you want students to shine in your classroom based on who they are?

Do you want students to just follow the directions so that you can control the environment?

Do you want students to learn first?

How will you ensure that you assess students' true knowledge bias free?

Think about a struggle you had growing up, how do you use this life lesson to empower your students?

Share out your reflections using #InspiringJY

AFFIRMATIONS

(Write, Draw, or Brainstorm ideas or thoughts here)

I am empowering voice and choice in the classroom while...

Jennifer delivers a **MUST-READ** for all educators, sharing easy-to-implement steps on intentionally building a classroom culture that supports each and every learner. *Inspiring JOY* opens your eyes to new ways to address character, excellence, and community in your classroom in this pivotal time in education when inclusion, relationships, connections, and authenticity are paramount.

Kari Pitstick, Middle Level Educator & Digital Content Coordinator, Teach Better Team

Lesson 12:

Skate Park - Experiential

> *"Traditional schools don't show you the world,*
> *they show you a bunch of careers"*
> *-Michelle Obama*

 ## Launch:

Teachers have the responsibility of introducing possibilities disguised as academic content. One of my all time favorite classes that I taught was 'remedial' math. Although I'm a reading specialist and have multiple degrees in reading, math was actually my favorite subject growing up. I've always been passionate about teaching others to love math as much as me. Math changed my life in so many positive ways. It gave me the confidence to become a teacher and stay in college. I frequently tutored other math students in high school and college. Despite all my formal training in reading, I jumped at the chance to teach math early in my career. Students were assigned to my math class because of: low test scores, failing grades, behavior concerns, or they just had a hard time in a traditional classroom.

For many learners math is just flat out difficult. Our brains are not hard wired to go on to the next level of math until we understand basic concepts. When I was teaching 5th grade, I had students who struggled with long division. No matter what we tried, they just did not get it. I would demonstrate different techniques, go over multiplication tables--heck I was willing to do cartwheels around the room, if I thought it'd help them. I tried everything possible. Then one day, they would just go, 'oh, I get it.' And they were ready to move on. It was like all of sudden, a switch was turned on in their brain. This is what math instruction is like--you show students 50 different ways to look at a problem and then all of the sudden their brain is ready to process the information. Explaining students a litany of ways to solve a problem requires patience and a bit of faith that it will all eventually click.

One year, I had a group of students that were exceptional in my 8th grade pre-algebra class. One particular learner in the class named Leslie was very intelligent but having a hard time understanding the concepts. She had a very low self-efficacy about her abilities. She believed she was stupid, and hadn't lived up to her older siblings, who were all in honors classes. Her low opinion of herself coupled with a diagnosed learning disability made for a tough road, as she expressed regular frustration that she wasn't getting it.

> CONTENT SPECIFIC ESTEEM DEFICITS CAN CAUSE LEARNERS TO DROWN IN THIS EDUCATIONAL QUICKSAND OF CONFUSION.

I noticed immediately that she was extremely intelligent but seemed to process information differently than most students. She wasn't a kid who could just take notes and do the problems. She had to think about concepts and really understand them to their core. Naturally, she fit right into my class as teaching outside the box is my speciality. Teaching outside the box isn't just about traditional teaching on the outside of said box, it's about REIMAGINING the box.

Maybe we should wear the box.

Poke holes in the box to let in new oxygen.

SURPRISE!

Let's jump in the box.

Let's stand on the box for a new perspective.

In her pre-algebra class, I remember laying on the desk to explain the concept of parallel and then demonstrating to them that I was parallel to the ground, before jumping on top of the desk to contrast the idea of perpendicular. Using my body to demonstrate math, shocked them a little, and in turn they never forgot those two concepts. My classes have always been very hands-on. There was never a dumb question--you were allowed to question me and ask why something happened and how we figured out a particular problem. I intentionally taught the students to challenge me on a daily basis as they were constantly asking me the origin of certain solving techniques or why I was using this method when an alternative method would work just as well. They learned shortcuts to solve problems because I wanted them to apply math toward their life, not just in an academic setting.

Back then, I had a group of learners that were obsessed with skateboards and they all, including Leslie had fingerboards. Capitalizing on their own interest, we set up a math course for them to solve the problems as they did tricks with their boards. For instance, they had to solve an equation to figure out slope before they were able to use their finger board on the jump. Students brought in real skateboards and taught me how to ride it in the middle of my class. This was one of the most student relevant projects that I have done in my 21 years of teaching. My students loved it!.

One day when we were about half way through the project, Leslie came in and said, "this is my favorite class!"

"I am glad that you are liking it", I said.

She immediately corrected me: "I am not just liking it, I actually understand math now. It's my favorite subject because I actually understand math. I get all the concepts and can figure out problems in my head, it has become part of who I am."

Processing her powerful declaration of affection for a subject that she previously hated left me with chills. I couldn't believe this student who usually barely scraped by in math with the help of her parents to pass the class, was now getting A's and having a lot of success. And that success was building confidence. Her parents heaped praise and admiration on me throughout the year as her math trajectory literally changed; but the truth is, Leslie was the one doing all the hard work.

STUDENT ACHIEVEMENT IS UNIMAGINABLY HIGH WHEN TEACHERS HELP REMOVE THE BARRIER OF SELF DOUBT.

In high school, she actually doubled up on math classes and took algebra and geometry the same year so that she could graduate having taken calculus. Hearing about her acceleration at math, and her newfound ability to succeed left me reflecting on what can happen when teachers apply experiential opportunities to help students find their passion and joy with learning new material.

> TEACHERS WHO INSPIRE JOY OPEN UP OPPORTUNITIES TO RE-CALIBRATE A STUDENT'S EDUCATIONAL PATH WHEN THEY INVEST TIME AND ENERGY INTO EXPERIENTIAL EXCELLENCE.

Experiential Math

 Expectations: Students don't just want projects that they can do. Teachers have an obligation to peak their interests by understanding their students' abilities and what they will need to be successful. This is all about relationships and helping to understand your students at a level that really gets to the core of what they need.

 Stuff: Experiential Projects should match your students interests and help them to understand the concepts that you are teaching.

 Skills: When you create authentic experiential learning for students they will learn responsible decision making, self-management, and social awareness.

Instruction/Activities:

If you hope to design a classroom that uses experiential learning on a regular basis you need to spend a lot of time at the beginning of the year on relationships. Building Character, Excellence, and Community can be your focus throughout your time with your students. For instance, if students don't have good character and the skills to work together or independently you can't have any of these fun experiences.

> THE SUCCESS OF EXPERIENTIAL LEARNING IS A FUNCTION OF A STUDENT'S SOFT SKILLS AND CHARACTER.

Step one

When you are thinking about doing any sort of experiential learning in your classroom answer these questions:
- What do your students need?
- Why are you doing this project?

- What are the non-academic concepts you are wanting to tease out and teach?
- Where might I infuse character building and social emotional learning?

A lot of times educators think about project based learning as the end result after the learning. You are creating something as a result of learning. But instead project based learning is the tool that we use to learn the concept.

Example:

When I set up the ramps and mini skate park in my room, I was thinking about what concepts my students were struggling with and how I could use something that they had interest in and teach them how it worked. They were able to solve problems and then test it out with their boards. When it was the wrong answer it was very apparent because the board didn't move like it was supposed to. They were able to see mistakes visually without me having to tell them. Learners discovered it on their own and came to logical conclusions on how to solve the problem based on something they knew a lot about. Learning something new under the umbrella of a high interest familiar experience elevates and accelerates internal connections.

Step Two

Make sure to budget in time for reflection. I suggest a journal, no matter what the subject. It might be digital, spiral, or a giant whiteboard; but, it's always present. It is used for reflection and to generate ideas and thoughts. This is crucial for students to truly understand their own thinking and as a resource to revisit what they did and how it will help them to solve other problems later.

 ## Close Intentionally:

TEACHERS' BIGGEST SUCCESS IS TO INSTILL SUCH PROFOUND CONFIDENCE IN THEIR STUDENTS' ABILITY TO LEARN THAT THEY IN TURN FEEL DRIVEN TO FORGE THEIR OWN EDUCATIONAL SUCCESS.

Educators tend to be quick to correct students' mistakes; sometimes choosing right answers over process. The real learning isn't in solving the problem in which the teacher puts in front of the student. It's to empower the students' mindset to find and attack problems that the teacher never even considered. If students have the wrong answer, encourage them to explain their thinking and how they came to their answer. Many times learners pinpoint their own mistakes by explaining their reasoning. Please give students time to think and process instead of just moving on to the next concept or giving them the answer. Student self-esteem is discovered in the moments between struggle and success.

<u>Opportunities:</u>

Experiential projects should be for everyone at your school. I've noticed that sometimes we gladly let honors students run with a passion project but limit struggling students in this exploration of learning. Ironically, these educators believe their toughest classes can't handle project based experiential learning because of behavior concerns. Very often behavior is communicating that our work lacks interest and engagement. Hands-on projects are exactly what struggling learners need. They are in desperate need of a departure from the traditional classroom.

> ALL LEARNERS NEED AND DESERVE OUTSIDE THE BOX OPPORTUNITIES TO FURTHER THEIR PASSION FOR THE CONTENT.

I've found that my struggling or at-risk learners needed experiential learning even more because they were kids that had a different way of thinking about the world. Traditional education wasn't working for them, so they needed a chance to learn from a different perspective. In my experience, support classes often rely on remedial type canned programs out there on the market that are very compliance driven, culturally biased, and are highly structured. Educators believe that by having students sit and work individually, in small groups, or larger groups rotating around these stations that learners will be inspired, motivated, and encouraged to explore content in which they already struggle with. This couldn't be further from the truth! We can't hold back our best ideas, lessons, and growth from our most struggling learners.

In my experience, students who are struggling in historically traditional schools desperately need learning through experience. They are the last students who should be sitting longer. They need to be learning through doing, talking, creating, teaming, and exploring. Build in movement, breaks, voice and choice. If we follow the research on attention spans, we recognize that students have about 2-3 minutes per year of age. Thus, a 10 year old has approximately 20-30 minutes of focus time. Students attention spans can vary greater, however; when they reach a flow state of passion based learning.

Furthermore, research studies support project-based learning over traditional instruction as a "powerful strategy to support long-term retention of content, performance in high-stakes tests, improves problem-solving and collaboration skills, and improves students' attitudes toward learning" (Strobel & Van Barneveld, 2009; Walker & Leary, 2009).

 **<u>Needs:</u>**

I remember sitting in a meeting for a student, with a group of teachers and administration sitting around discussing how to help the kiddo. He was really struggling in his classes and had been unable to find success; however, he had high test scores. We were discussing many options, and someone said,

"I think that he should be in Jen's math class because he'll find success there".

At that time, my math class (basically tier 2-3 before that existed), had become a place to put students that weren't successful in traditional classes, regardless of academic skill. Another teacher, whom I respected a lot, fired back with:

"We can't just give them all to Jen when we can't figure out how to help them. We need to figure out what she is doing so that we can be better teachers, not just hand them off to her to fix".

When colleagues recognize the work you're doing and actively seek to learn from you, it's undeniable that your experiential efforts are paying big student dividends.

 Self-Reflection:

What's one thing you're going to change about the experiential projects you're currently doing in your classroom?

Reflecting back on your time as a student...can you recall a cool lesson that really motivated you to learn? What was it specifically that ignited your passion to learn?

Share out your reflections using #InspiringJOY

AFFIRMATIONS

(Write, Draw, or Brainstorm ideas or thoughts here)

EXPERIENTIAL LEARNING LOOKS LIKE...

Jennifer's LESSICONS framework is a **MUCH NEEDED** approach in the classroom to help educators introduce and seamlessly integrate SEL practices that are certain to help in developing the whole child and inspire joy. Educators will appreciate the relatable stories that Jennifer shares in order to highlight each aspect of the framework and no doubt be inspired to connect to their own stories in order to generate connection and joy from an authentic place, and ultimately to create not only joy-filled classrooms, but joy-filled communities.

Athea Davis, Mindfulness Educator

LESSON 13:

JUVIE-EPIC

 **Launch:**

As a second grade student teacher, if you would have told me that a year later I'd be watching my 6 foot tall 7th grade high ACEs student live out his wildest family traumas on an episode of the outrageous Jerry Springer television show—well, I would have thought you were crazy...

When I was in college, I was absolutely driven to get a degree in Elementary Education (K-8) and K-12 Reading. My intention all through college was to get a job in 2nd grade or be a reading specialist, focused on elementary kiddos. Perhaps, I'd be willing to go up to 3rd grade, or might be willing to go down to Kindergarten. However, I could declare with 100% certainty that my career path would land somewhere between K-3. I loved the little ones and was fueled to teach reading.

After graduating from college, moving back to my hometown, and getting married, I was eager to get started in a classroom. Because my husband was still in school getting his masters in counseling, I needed a full time job with benefits as I'd be the one working while he finished school. Naturally, I applied for various elementary jobs, but being late August nothing was working out. Ironically, I was moving into my apartment and the principal of one of the middle schools happened to be my neighbor. In passing, she mentioned that she had an opening for a 7th grade math position and wondered if I might be interested in applying. I never wanted to teach middle school, but I needed a job and thought, WHY NOT! I nailed the interview and a week later found myself as the brand new 22 year old math teacher in a 6-12 school.

Truth be told, I looked like one of the high schoolers on the same campus. In fact, my baby face got interrogated for a hall pass on more than one occasion by adult supervisors. My first year in education was a whirlwind of crazy experiences that really helped me become a better teacher. Looking back, I fell in love with hormonal and smelly middle schoolers, desperate to find themselves while they teeter tottered back and forth between child and young adult.

I had one particular student that 1st year who I will never forget. Honestly, there's a part of me that will always worry about Tom. Tom was a huge 6 foot tall, 7th grade man-child who easily weighed 200 pounds. He redefined 'rough around the edges' and definitely looked older than me, in all my 5 foot 4 inch glory! BUT, he was a giant teddy bear on the inside, who was kind, and loved being in my class.

Unfortunately, Tom's world outside of my classroom was unbelievably challenging. He came from a single parent, high poverty, drug infused home. There were family ties to gangs and readily available access to weapons. Tom would often find himself kicked out of class or in conflict with peers and adults, while he fought to hide his pain from the world. His family drama even managed to play out on national television that year.

Those of you who are old enough will remember a show called Jerry Springer. As a salacious tabloid-ish talk show, Springer was a revolutionarily trashy program with fist fights, screaming and paternity tests all captured on camera. The 15 minutes of fame couldn't have been worth the embarrassment that Tom and his family suffered as he returned to school after airing dirty laundry for viewers to witness.

> *"Be curious, not judgmental."*
> *-Walt Whitman*

One day, Tom confided in me about all of the time that he was spending in juvenile detention; but his truth rocked me in a way I will never forget. He shared with me that he liked being in juvie because it was quiet, he could read and study, and he got 3 meals each day. He went on to explain how they always had a guard there to watch over them, a consistent routine that he could follow. According to Tom, other than MY CLASSROOM--it was the most stable place in his life.

I was lucky enough to have Tom for 2 years in a row (7th/8th grade). During an August planning meeting for his 8th grade year, Tom and his counselor shared with me that he requested to have me in math again because he felt I was the one person who made him feel safe. Additionally, he mentioned how I was really good at explaining concepts that he normally wouldn't understand, and that I wouldn't judge him. I think he knew I genuinely cared about him.

"If I can't have Mrs. Appel as a teacher then I might as well just go back to Juvie."

Tom melted my heart as he taught me way more in those 2 years than I ever taught him.

Being willing to actively SEARCH for a child's inner awesomeness provides students with HOPE. Hope in themselves. Hope in education. Hope in their own future...And hope leads directly to belief!

Making an EPIC experience for students.

 Expectations: Through the lens of an EPIC mindset you are able to create an experience in your classroom that students desperately desire.

 Stuff: Essential, Personalized, Intentional and Curious

 Skills: The Orbit of Silence, teaches students self-awareness, self-management, and responsible decision making.

Instruction/Activities:

When I think about Tom there were a lot of staff members operating with a negative desirability bias to view him in a certain light that caused him to behave in an unhealthy self-fulfilling prophecy of classroom delinquency. They were afraid of him, because of the way he looked or the way he acted out. There were a lot of jokes from staff about his family's appearance on an obscene talk show, (that was no fault of his) and he was given judgement for those actions. This was a case of a student who's presentation of himself to others was not the real person. He was having to put on a front so that he could survive each day. He wore this protective armor in the way that an animal in the wild might strike first to prevent getting hurt.

[*Reflecting on Tom, reminds me of a time my dog Ginger growled and barked at another dog on a walk. It was such a strange sight as she never opened her mouth and was the sweetest most gentle dog. However, the dog was trying to attack her sister Maya and bite her. Thus, gentle Ginger started acting tough to keep the danger away from her sister. She was in full on protection mode*].

In many ways, that's how Tom lived his life each day. He was always in protection mode, just trying to make it through each anticipated negative experience. The only way that he knew how to survive was to show overwhelming aggression towards others; and perhaps, that would help land him back in his safe space: juvenile detention. When you create an EPIC environment for students you ensure that they don't have to put up their guard and protect themselves. Instead, thoughtful educators provide students with the freedom to BE themselves.

Essential: With every single lesson, unit and year long study as a teacher you have to identify the essentials. Some teachers might think everything is essential. Do I have to do it all? NO! You have to narrow down your focus and really pick the most critical pieces that need to be covered in your lessons. Educators can use a variety of paths to arrive at the learning target. For instance, as an ELA teacher I am always looking at multiple ways that they can practice the writing process which doesn't require a traditional essay. We might write a blog, a personal narrative, a thank-you letter, or a tweet with limited characters. The writing process is essential but that doesn't mean students have to write multiple paragraph essays to achieve the writing goal. Students need experience writing in many different modalities.

Another essential is SEL. Teachers can build in short amounts of time to work on relationships and teach those "soft skills." If I hadn't taken the time to ask Tom about his experience in Juvie and what he was feeling, I never would have learned his story or understood what he really needed from my class. He was starving for someone to care for him, and help him regulate his emotions. Plus, he needed food! Keeping snacks for him in my cupboard became as essential as learning integers and fractions. He was taught to grab a snack during my class (without asking) to make sure that he was ready to be a learner.

Personalized: One of the reasons that Tom liked to be in my class is that it was personalized to meet his needs. Systems like The Grid Method by Chad Ostrowski provide teachers with a wonderful framework of personalizing lesson planning to meet the needs of a student. Educators tend to give everyone the exact same task or assignment when in reality we hate when others don't recognize our own individual needs, skills, and pace. We are all unique and need to have the autonomy to choose what works best for our situation.

Teaching history taught me to be very creative. History has a lot of information that needs to be absorbed by the students in order to later synthesize and really look at the core issues, while analyzing what they learned. In my history classes, I changed my way of thinking and no longer have a requirement for note taking. [*I know...I'm pretty sure a few rockstar history teachers officially stopped reading my book*]. Students need some way to keep track of bits of information to be able to analyze it later. However, learners can use traditional note taking, shorthand, cornell note style, sketch notes OR they can simply look at my presentation online and follow along and just listen. I tell my students that they are able to decide for themselves what they need and how they need to get the information.

Here's the deep dark secret that many of us teachers are afraid to admit. The facts, dates, and names in history are FAR LESS ESSENTIAL than being able to apply the information.

For instance, all the relevant historical facts and figures in Ancient Egypt are readily available to anyone with access to the internet. By boiling down to the essential skills, educators are primed to personalize classroom experiences within a whole child framework that focus on bigger ideas: character traits, community building, empathy and tolerance.

> WHEN TEACHERS TAKE THE TIME TO INTENTIONALLY FOCUS ON WHAT CONTENT MATTERS MOST...LEARNING GOES BEYOND BASIC UNDERSTANDING AND INSTEAD RESULTS IN LIFE CHANGING APPLICATION.

Sometimes, students need personalized support regulating their behavior. These students may bring emotional baggage from home, hallway, or history that impedes their ability to be an immediate learner. Very often these students' mind, body, and heart become misaligned during these moments of deregulation. Thus, returning to a mindful head space ready to be a successful learner can be quite challenging. One strategy I created years ago was a concept I call the Orbit of Silence (OS). The OS builds in an individualized moment of silence for students to get ready to become learners. For instance, Tom was given a special oversized desk with a teacher chair to fit his unique middle school size. Each day, he'd come in, he knew he had the first 5-10 minutes of class to collect his thoughts, steady his emotions, grab a snack, and prepare to be present in my class. While other students might be busily working on an entry task, Tom was given quiet time to get ready.

> WHEN WE ALLOW SPACE BETWEEN EMOTION AND THOUGHT WE PROVIDE STUDENTS THE OPPORTUNITY TO LEAN INTO JOY.

During this time, I would quietly drop off a stack of paper to be shredded on his desk. As you can imagine, all day, I would store up anything that 'needed' to be shredded and save it for Tom to take care of. The physical action of ripping paper up for me was an unspoken but fully agreed upon classroom job that permitted Tom to get micro-frustrations released while feeling helpful to me. It was a beautiful outlet for a kid who absolutely would have laughed off a stress ball, fidget, or anxiety putty. Nevertheless, he eagerly awaited the opportunity to get rid of my ridiculous quantity of 'necessary' shredding.

Orbit of Silence

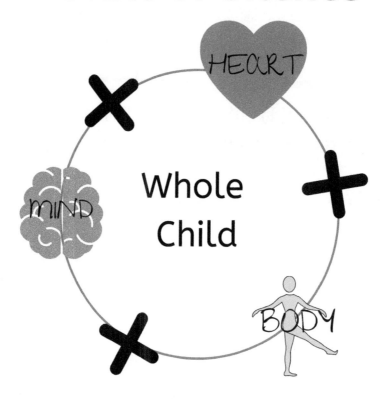

Mind + Heart + Body =
Whole Child = Pursuing JOY

Rather than being peppered with questions or a steady stream of reminders to get back on task, Tom was actively encouraged to decompress for a few minutes. Giving him the space to allow his mind, body, and heart to realign, ensured that he was able to give me his absolute best. The results of the Orbit of Silence with Tom, and countless learners over the years, has proved to be a real difference maker in academic production through this agreed upon emotional landing space.

The Orbit of Silence is reinforced by a litany of psychological and biological research. Daniel Siegel refers to students' unregulated state of entry into the classroom as their *"downstairs brain"* (Siegel & Bryson, 2012). Tom's downstairs brain would often trigger a survival thriving reaction-- flight-fight-freeze. And as Pete Hall explains, students benefit immensely from a culture of safety that includes: *"safety, predictability, and consistency"* (Hall, 2020). The Orbit of Silence was quite literally changing Tom's brain chemistry after the hallway had flooded him with adrenaline and cortisol.

INTENTIONAL TEACHERS CAN POSITIVELY FLIP A STUDENTS ABILITY TO LEARN BY REDUCING BUILT UP STRESS, FEAR, AND ANXIETY.

Intentional: In *Award Winning Culture*, Appel explains how he learned the need for intentionality within the helping confines of the counseling space. His "tissue lesson" reminds readers that successful educators must break actions down to their smallest parts to truly create a special experience for our learners.

In my classroom, I realized that our room's appearance needed to intentionally meet students where they are. One summer, I came into my room and took all of the posters down from my wall. I stripped it almost completely bare, only leaving a few school brand specific words up in large letters, #wildcatnation, #characterstrong, and #chooselove (Norlin, Kraft). I took everything else down in an effort to allow my students to hang their work and cultivate a classroom unique to them. No longer was MY classroom mine. No longer were they simply guests in my space. It was OUR working space! For the first time, in my career, room 615 belonged to my students. They were able to hang up their projects, decorate with pictures of their class, or photos and drawings they were proud of.

The blank walls in my classroom

CLASSROOM WALLS ARE A CANVAS TO EXPRESS STUDENTS' VISUAL HOPES AND DREAMS.

Later in the year, as our class culture begins to become stronger, I make mistakes intentionally to create a discussion in my classroom. Civil discourse is such a powerful skill that our learners will need in their future. Sometimes, I will use a pronoun the wrong way in a sentence and see if they catch it.

This tells me several things:
- Are they really understanding how to use pronouns (formative assessment)?
- If they catch it, why is it wrong?
- What is the reasoning behind this mistake?
- How do they handle explaining my error to me?

Being able to see their own learning from multiple perspectives is an advanced skill in reaching for empathic excellence.

Curiosity: In *Future Driven*, Geurin talks about allowing students to ask the question: what if? In education we seem to think of that phrase...***WHAT IF***...as bad words. Teachers feel inherent pressure to get through curriculum and don't always feel freedom to stop every few minutes and answer these probing follow up questions. I remember distinctly in the beginning of my career telling students: '*STOP with the What If questions*!' But stifling student inquiry is like dragging an anchor at the shallow end of the lake of student learning. You may eventually reach your classroom goals but you're destined to scare away all the fish.

> *"If you want to fly, you have to give up the things that weigh you down."*
> -Toni Morrison

Well, everything changed for me after reading Geurin's book. What if questions are no longer the things that weigh me down. They act as a rudder to the ship I'm co-navigating with my students. I now invite, cajole, and even celebrate learners asking those critical questions.

> ## CLARIFICATION OF THOUGHT IS WHERE THE REAL MAGIC IN LEARNING HAPPENS.

God bless kindergarten teachers. They are the most patient people I've ever met. They always take the time to thoroughly answer these follow up questions. But somewhere in between kindergarten and middle school we stop having patience for it and begin to see these inquiries as a distraction. We need to get back to the original thought of fostering curiosity in our learners. Now, I love WHAT IF questions in my classroom. They almost always lead to the richest discussions and the opportunity to crystalize learning.

 ## Close Intentionally:

When I think back about Tom, I still find myself worried about him nearly 20 years later. I know that he was safe and successful in my sphere of influence during those formative middle school years. I made a difference in his life and I hope that he thinks back about his time in my class with fond memories, knowing he had a teacher who created a safe learning space because she truly cared about him.

 ## Opportunities:

Lessons can NOT always be the same for every student. I totally understand that this is hard to do in the micromanaged educational world we live in with testing, evaluations, mandated curriculum, and standards. But it's critical to be creative while staying in the box. Providing your students the ability to reach excellence in the classroom means being willing to be truly curious about their individual needs as a learner.

> EDUCATIONAL SUCCESS IS AN INDIVIDUALIZED GROWTH JOURNEY RATHER THAN A ONE SIZE FITS ALL LEARNING DESTINATION.

 ## Needs:

I knew I had achieved an EPIC classroom for Tom when he shared how my room was the only safe space outside of Juvie in his life. If behavior is the way our students communicate needs, I think students are gifting us evaluative information about our success in creating essential, personalized, intentional, and curious classrooms EVERYDAY!

Are you listening? Are you reflecting? Are you acting on that regular communication of student needs?

 ## Self-Reflection:

How might you use an EPIC lens to create excellent learning moments for an at-risk student?

In what ways, will you personalize an upcoming lesson to better serve your students?

Are you intentionally making mistakes and building in unspoken classroom procedures to meet your learners where they're at by modeling excellent character traits?

Think about a student you've had and what he or she taught you. How might you apply that experience to create a culture of excellence for future learners?

Share out your reflections using #InspiringJ🍎Y

AFFIRMATIONS

(Write, Draw, or Brainstorm ideas or thoughts here)

An E.P.I.C. classroom feels...

In her outstanding sequel to *Award Winning Culture*, Jennifer Appel shines as she shares her personal and professional experiences in **POWERFUL** and practical lessons for her fellow educators. Appel demonstrates her commitment to her craft by being vulnerable, reflective, and encouraging while modeling how to create "joy-filled classrooms that have **LIFE-ALTERING** consequences" for both students and educators. *Inspiring JOY* challenges educators to meet students where they are, identify their strengths and talents, and empower students to use their voice to become part of the learning process.

Mariah Rackley, Ed.D., Award-Winning Principal, Cedar Crest Middle School

Excellence Lesson Plan

Excellence -- Will you do your very best?

 LAUNCH:

Can someone tell me what time management is? Why is it good to manage your time?

 EXPECTATIONS:

- Students will learn about time management and how to organize activities in the most efficient manner.
- Students will learn about their own character by understanding if they can persevere through a challenge and identify the grit required to complete the task.

 STUFF:

- Planner
- Access to a sink to wash their hands (maybe more than one)
- Locker

 SKILLS:

Students will learn Self-Awareness, Self-Management, and Responsible Decision Making.

INSTRUCTION/ACTIVITES:

- Teacher Note:
  - The purpose of this activity is to teach the students about time management and perseverance through a fun activity.
  - The goal of the activity is to have the students reflect on their own character and what skills they currently possess.
  - This activity will also give you insight into your students and the ones that are willing to do anything to get an activity done and those that will just give up because of the difficulty.
  - This activity is not intended as a competition and does not need to actually be completed. Students are just experiencing the idea of time management.
- Students will be told that they will have 3 tasks to get done in a certain amount of time. They are not allowed to start until you start the timer in the front of the room.
- Your 3 tasks are:
  - Fill out your planner for your class.
  - Wash your hands.
  - Go to your locker and open it and bring an item into class.
  - Note: These can be any 3 tasks as long as it requires them to physically move around and have a very limited amount of time to accomplish.

128

CHALLENGE

You will have 2 MINUTES to complete these tasks:

1. Log-in to your Chromebook, open your digital planner, and fill out today's task.
2. Wash your hands.
3. Go to your locker and bring back any item.

Rules:
Silence, Walking, and Respect

- THE STUDENTS WILL HAVE 2 MINUTES TO GET ALL OF THIS DONE AND THE RULES ARE SILENCE, WALKING, AND RESPECT. MAKE SURE YOU HAVE A TIMER DISPLAYED ON THE BOARD TO LET THEM KNOW HOW MUCH TIME THEY HAVE LEFT.
- HAVE THE STUDENTS START THE ACTIVITY AND PAY ATTENTION TO WHO IS DOING WHAT AND WHY YOU THINK THEY ARE DOING IT. THIS IS IMPORTANT TO WATCH FOR THOSE STUDENTS THAT ARE JUST SITTING AND THOSE THAT ARE HURRYING AROUND TRYING TO GET EVERYTHING DONE. ALSO, TO ADD PRESSURE MAKE SURE THAT YOU TELL THEM THE TIME EVERY 30 SECONDS.
- WHEN THE TIME RUNS OUT, FACILITATE A DISCUSSION ASKING THE FOLLOWING QUESTIONS:
  - WHAT DID YOU DO FIRST? WAS IT WHAT YOU ORIGINALLY HAD PLANNED?
  - IF YOU CHANGED YOUR PLAN, WHY?
  - WHAT DID YOU NOTICE ABOUT HOW OTHERS WERE FINISHING THE TASKS?
  - HOW MANY OF YOU GAVE UP? HOW MANY OF YOU WERE OVERWHELMED?
  - HOW WOULD IT HAVE CHANGED THINGS IF YOU WERE GIVEN A MINUTE TO COME UP WITH A PLAN?
  - DID YOU LEARN ANYTHING FROM THE ORDER IN WHICH YOU DID THINGS?
  - DID YOU TAKE ANY SHORTCUTS AND THEN PAY FOR IT LATER? (I.E. NOT DRYING YOUR HANDS AFTER WASHING THEM AND THEN NOT ABLE TO OPEN YOUR LOCKER BECAUSE YOUR HANDS ARE WET)
  - IF WE DID THIS ACTIVITY AGAIN NOW, WHAT WOULD YOU DO DIFFERENTLY? WOULD YOU BE MORE/LESS SUCCESSFUL? WHY?
  - HOW MANY OF YOU STOPPED TO HELP A CLASSMATE, OFFER A SMILE OR WORK TOGETHER? WHY OR WHY NOT?
  - WHY DID WE DO THIS LESSON?
  - HOW MIGHT IDENTITY, CULTURAL BACKGROUND, OR PHYSICAL OBSTACLES INFLUENCE OR IMPACT SOMEONE'S PARTICIPATION?
  - WHAT DID IT TEACH YOU ABOUT YOUR CHARACTER?

CLOSE INTENTIONALLY:

- DISCUSSION:
  - WHEN WE THINK ABOUT WHAT WE ARE DOING AND MAKE A PLAN, THINGS GO MUCH SMOOTHER. YOU ALSO NEED TO THINK ABOUT YOUR STRENGTHS AND WEAKNESSES AND WHAT YOU WILL WANT TO WORK ON THIS YEAR TO HELP IMPROVE SOME OF THOSE SKILLS.

 OPPORTUNITIES:

- FOR ELEMENTARY SCHOOL, YOU CAN HAVE THE STUDENTS PICK UP ONE PIECE OF GARBAGE, WRITE A SENTENCE ON A PIECE OF PAPER (OR MAYBE JUST A WORD), AND THEN HAVE THEM TOUCH THE WALL OPPOSITE THEM.
- FOR HIGH SCHOOL YOU CAN HAVE THEM TEXT A COMPLIMENT TO A FRIEND, DO A COMPLEX MATH PROBLEM, AND THEN CREATE A CALENDAR APPOINTMENT ON THEIR COMPUTER OR PHONE.

 NEEDS:

- A GREAT FOLLOW UP TO THIS ACTIVITY IS HAVING THE STUDENTS CREATE A SCHEDULE FOR THEIR WEEK. WHEN CAN THEY GET THINGS DONE AND WHAT IS THE BEST TIME OF DAY FOR THEM TO WORK AND BE EFFICIENT.
- FAMILY CONNECTION: ONE OF THE WAYS TO CONTINUE THE WORK OF STRIVING FOR EXCELLENCE IS TO INVOLVE FAMILIES IN THE PROCESS. HERE IS AN EXAMPLE POST THAT YOU COULD PRINT AND SEND HOME WITH KIDS, POST ON SOCIAL MEDIA AND YOUR LEARNING MANAGEMENT SYSTEM, OR SEND IN AN EMAIL.

EXCELLENCE

WILL YOU DO YOUR VERY BEST?

In class today, we did an activity to help us learn about time management, perseverance and doing our best.

Here are some reflection questions for you to discuss as a family:

- How do you manage your time to accomplish all of your goals?
- What does it mean in our family to do your very best?
- What does it mean to persevere in our family?

SELF-REFLECTION:

- REFLECT ABOUT YOUR CLASS:
  - DID YOU SEE ANYONE REFUSE TO DO THE ACTIVITY? IF YOU HAVE ANYONE THAT DIDN'T DO IT, THEY MIGHT STRUGGLE WITH PERSEVERANCE OR MAYBE ANXIETY AND THEY WERE OVERWHELMED. OR THERE MAY BE CULTURAL IMPLICATIONS THAT YOU WEREN'T AWARE OF.
  - DID YOU HAVE ANY STUDENTS TRY TO SKIP A STEP, LIKE DRYING THEIR HANDS AND THEN THEY COULDN'T OPEN THEIR LOCKER?
  - DID YOU HAVE STUDENTS THAT PLANNED OUT THE WHOLE 90 SECONDS BEFORE YOU STARTED THE TIMER? THESE ARE STUDENTS THAT NEED VERY CLEAR INSTRUCTIONS AHEAD OF TIME AND NEED TO SEE THE BIGGER VISION.

UNIT 3: COMMUNITY

A strong community is the essential life blood of our educational work. But how do we SHAPE our communities to answer the all important question: What Will YOU Do for Others TODAY? In section three of, *Award Winning Culture*, Hans breaks down a handful of critical points which includes: Social Media, House Rules, Authentic Branding, Personal Outreach, and Experience. Through these 5 elements, school-wide leaders learn how to become masterful school storytellers with a unified WHY rooted in serving others, while also amplifying connection, feeling, and school spirit.

Higher institutions and employers are begging for K-12 educators to focus on these critical soft skills. For instance, "92% of surveyed executives say problem solving, emotional regulation, and communication are equal to or more important than technical skills" (Casel.org). Communities experience increased economic mobility, reduced poverty, and better lifetime outcomes. Simple put, for every $1 invested in this whole learner work, society receives $11 in return.

However, true societal defining culture and climate comes about through a grassroots effort of awesomeness that originates within the classroom. And as teachers, we have the most impactful hand in building a unified cohesive cohort out of these individual cast of characters. In Unit 3, we'll zero in on how teachers hold the most influence to shaping the school community of joyful whole learners.

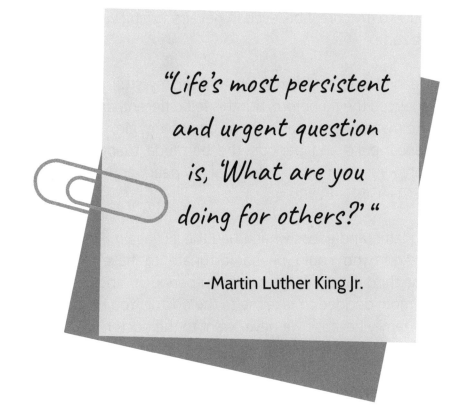

"Life's most persistent
and urgent question
is, 'What are you
doing for others?'"

-Martin Luther King Jr.

LESSON 14:
ENDO-SOCIAL MEDIA

 **Launch:**

Picking out my most embarrassing middle school experience is like asking Magic Johnson to pick his favorite all time basketball assist. There are so many, how do you even choose?

As I squirmed in my chair, looking across my small wooden desk at my blue binder covered in my own puke, I couldn't help but wonder...what's happening to me?

All morning I had experienced a difficult time concentrating. Granted, it was the last day of school but I couldn't shake this sick to my stomach feeling foreshadowing an afternoon of humiliation. I was an excessively compliant kid and always believed that athletes just needed to tough it out. To my core, I believed in never showing weakness and that school was a no complaining zone.

NOPE, not today. I leaned over and threw up all over my stuff to the side of my desk. Certainly, I had experienced the flu before, but this felt different, uncontrollable, and much more painful. To make matters worse, as a young adolescent girl, I had literally just started my period. Adolescence, puke and periods--the bermuda triangle of agony! Yeah me! Ending my year by throwing up in class, in front of my peers and starting my period all in the same day: LUCKIEST---GIRL---EVER!

Fast forward a month later, and guess what, I had the 'flu' again. First of all, who gets the flu a second time? And, who could be so fortunate to have it coincide with their period...AGAIN?! By the third month of having the flu-period combo coupled with the most excruciating pain, my mom decided to take me to the doctor. You have to understand, this was a big move in our family because we never went to the doctor. The physician talked to us and pretended to listen to my symptoms and then told me to basically toughen up.

"Sweetie...women get periods and you're being dramatic and overly sensitive," he condescendly shared.

134

Despite leaving the doctor's office resolved to trust the expert, my symptoms never went away. In fact, they only got worse. My second doctor visit resulted in me learning that I had a "low pain tolerance." I had no idea I was such a weak minded individual but luckily for me I was prescribed the miracle drug of extra strength tylenol [cue the sarcasm gif here]. The doctor went on to suggest I might need to see a psychologist because the 'pain' was all in my head.

Feeling helplessly in physical torment while being informed that you're crazy is a healthy combination to impose on a young pre-teen girl. I began to confirm the notion that all girls deal with acute stabbing pain, shortness of breath, diarrhea, nausea, and vomiting. No big deal. This is what it means to be a woman...RIGHT?

For many years, I put up with the pain and bloating by reminding myself that this was all in my head. You can imagine what kind of effects this would have on my adolescent brain and self-esteem as I ploughed through this horrible internal turmoil. Each month, suddenly being unable to fit into my regular clothes before miraculously transforming into my normal size 2 weeks later. [I became so adept at overcoming pain that in high school I ran 2 weeks on a stress fracture while breaking a personal record on my 200 sprint. I'd learn later that my pain threshold was unusually high as the athletic accomplishments I was achieving on my broken down body were truly remarkable].

Transitioning to college meant I had a chance to meet new doctors who tried their unsuccessful cocktail of pharmaceuticals. With each new doctor visit, a sense of hope would fill my body before a couple months later being welcomed back to undeserving suffering. In my early 20's, I was unable to eat for extended windows of time. I would throw up if I tried to eat anything, or for that matter drink water. My husband and I had a rule that if I went 7 days without being able to eat, he'd force me to go to the emergency room.

During the school day I quietly struggled to survive teaching. The teaching part was great, but the once monthly attacks had deteriorated into almost continuous health issues. I had a garbage can outside my classroom with a packet of gum tucked under the bag. I would have to run out of the room to quietly throw up and then shove a piece of cinnamon gum in my mouth before walking back in with a friendly smile ready to dazzle my middle school audience. I was in constant pain and sick all of the time. Throughout all this ordeal, I still thought I must just be a wimp and unable to handle anything. I believed that if I convinced myself the pain wasn't real, I could make it through the day.

Finally, after a particularly horrific emergency room visit, the doctor couldn't find anything wrong and again was playing it off like I was crazy. I remember her asking me what my pain level was 1-10, and I was always in denial about my pain, so I said about an 8, which for most people is probably about a 50. All I remember is Hans getting so mad at the doctor and sharing that if my wife says that she is an 8 she is in extreme pain and that she needed to do something. Although this doctor said there was nothing she could find; eventually she sent me to another doctor to follow up.

Come to find out after 15 years of dealing with pain, I was diagnosed with Stage 4 endometriosis...

[Endometriosis occurs when tissue called endometrium is found outside its normal location, which results in inflammation. The disease affects 1 in 10 women aged 12-52 - an estimated 20 million women worldwide. Endometriosis is one of the leading causes of infertility and does not currently have a cure. The disease can impact all aspects of life and the symptoms may be so severe that individuals miss school, work, sports, or social events (Endofund.org)].

Truth be told this diagnosis while initially a relief did not result in much sustainable change. Multiple surgeons took turns playing god with my reproductive organs while downplaying my experiences. 3 doctors and 5 more surgeries later, I finally found a real specialist that truly understood the pathology of endo. In my late 30's, I finally had an expert who couldn't cure my disease but could help me create a plan to manage my symptoms.

Thanks to the confusion, shame, and embarrassment of uncovering both a diagnosis and treatment for my years of chronic illness I really never shared much about my story with others. I told a few close friends and my family, but I never complained and hid much of my daily trials and tribulations from even those closest to me. For years, I didn't believe people would understand and that my story wasn't worth sharing with them. I've learned that the average woman with endo, takes 15 years to receive a proper diagnosis and that my story is far too similar to countless other women.

These years of trauma have reinforced to me that telling our story helps others to truly understand our reality. For years, doctors told my health and wellness story. Friends, family, and colleagues told my story about not being a parent or decisions on strict dietary needs.

Teachers find themselves in a familiar disadvantaged role of letting parents, politicians, and society tell our classroom stories. No one knows all the magic happening in your room if you choose to keep it a secret. Furthermore, people will never know how to help you as a teacher, if you don't put a voice to your educational needs. It's time for teachers to take back the narrative on sharing the amazingness, challenges, and barriers happening in our own classrooms. Additionally, if you're feeling overwhelmed or in need of support and guidance in your role on the front lines of education, I implore you: SHARE YOUR STORY! There are so many amazing people who are ready to celebrate and support you.

> **TEACHERS THRIVING IN A JOYFUL CLASSROOM MAKE INTENTIONAL TIME, ENERGY, AND EFFORT TO SHARE THEIR STUDENT'S EDUCATIONAL STORY OUTSIDE THE 4 WALLS OF THE CLASSROOM.**

Sharing your story.

 Expectations: Teachers will regularly share their own classroom story.

 Stuff: Teachers use social media/platforms to share their individual classroom story with colleagues, leaders, parents, and community by finding universal belief that what's happening in our school is truly exceptional. Additionally, when we're brave enough to share our classroom story all other schools benefit.

 Skills: When you are able to tell your classroom story, students become very social aware of what is happening outside of the classroom.

Instruction/Activities:

> *"If you don't tell your story, someone else will."*
> *-Beth Houf*

Teachers have a chance to ensure others know the awesomeness happening in their classrooms. Social media is a great avenue for teachers to communicate their educational narrative. Rather than using social media for doomscolling large quantities of negative online news at once to the detriment of our own mental health; teachers can harness its power for incredible optimism and hope by sharing education's elicor of excellence. Intentional social media users avoid mindlessly scrolling--instead actively asking themselves: How will this content, connection, or community help me and my learners grow?

When teachers fail to take advantage of technological platforms like these, parents, colleagues, and community simply fill in their perceived details based on their childhood experiences, mass media representation, or political perceptions. The same is true of our colleagues. I've had many teachers over the years criticize my classroom for a variety of reasons. Kids love being in my room; and, undoubtedly, jealousy breeds contempt.

Some educators have told me: 'Oh, well you are the easy teacher, or your students are just taking advantage of you.' Occasionally, I'm informed that I'm not teaching the curriculum verbatim, following the book closely enough and that my kids won't be prepared to excel academically. And you know what, when I first started teaching, I let other teachers tell my story and it became my own. This form of gaslighting transforms innovative teachers into being afraid of professional risk-taking through social contagion. Toxic school culture is a breeding ground for unhealthy emotional contagion.

I started giving tricky assignments and grading based on something I didn't believe in, so that I wouldn't be viewed as the "easy" teacher. But that didn't work. It just made me into what I thought others wanted, and sadly the students suffered because of it. Similar to dealing with Endo, it took me a while to find the courage to share my learners' truth.

> FEAR OF JUDGEMENT PROVIDES A WHISPER OF SHAME INTO OUR EDUCATIONAL SOUL; WHEREAS, CLASSROOM TRUTH BECOMES A PARADE OF STUDENTS' LEARNING TO DROWN OUT SELF DOUBT.

The stories that others create about us are not true but can become wide perception if we don't open up the doors for others to peek into our edu-spaces. I constantly post pictures and videos on social media from classroom events, activities, and general awesomeness around the school. I love telling the story of my kids and how they are amazing. Frankly, I don't want another human being to miss out on the incredibleness of what happens in education. I love inviting adults into my classroom to witness the learning magic in real time. And guess what? Our kids benefit from this openness more than anyone!

> When a fellow teacher criticizes your room for being easy, they are essentially communicating to your students that they aren't working hard. They're insinuating that the learners might be just sliding by. This untruth isn't fair to the students and the hard work that they are putting in.

Telling your classroom story also builds powerful relationships with parents and community members who may never have the opportunity to step foot into your physical world. The school to home success pipeline from these parent/teacher cohesions is astronomical on student achievement. When parents sincerely understand what's happening at school, the rich follow-up discussions and academic partnerships help us reach incredible academic heights of JOY. Teachers who tell their classroom story with social media or other learning management platforms facilitate all stakeholders being on the same page to support a learner's needs.

 ## Close Intentionally:

When you are wondering if you should tell your story, think about my example earlier about my struggles and how life would have been so much better had I stood up for myself and shared my truth. When people understand your classroom story, they will line up to support the work you're doing.

 ## Opportunities:

If your district doesn't allow social media, then you can send out a regular newsletter to parents and community members. Plus, there are tons of non-social media platforms to share out. Remind, Class Dojo, and Seesaw can all provide ample opportunity to reach families. Teachers can post cool pictures on bulletin boards in the hallway for others to see what you are doing in your classroom. Invite the local media in to do a story. Ask parents or office staff to come be a guest judge for a class project. The point is...we must open up our lesson plan book for our communities. The work you and your students are doing is outstandly life-changing. Be proud of your students and what they are accomplishing!

 ## Needs:

I remember a teacher was criticizing me in the hallway and saying that I was the easy teacher, and a student happened to be around the corner and heard this teacher's criticism, they came around the corner and said,

"Mrs. Appel is NOT an easy teacher. She is actually the toughest teacher I have had. She pushes us everyday. Now, she is the nicest teacher also, so I love coming to her class and it doesn't feel like work, but she is NOT an easy teacher."

Obviously, I didn't need to be defended by this sweet-hearted student. But when you've created such a tight learning culture and taken the time to empower students to share their learning they end up taking such personal initiative to viscerally perpetuate your award winning culture to everyone around them. Pretty soon, you're not the only one sharing the classroom story.

 ## Self-Reflection:

How do you share your story with your students? Your Principal? Your Peers? Your Students' Families? Your Community?

What's one way you can begin to tell your classroom story this week?

How might you live your own excellence and build a stronger community by sharing your own story with people in your life?

How do you motivate students to share their own story?

Can you think of a time that you failed to share your story in your personal life? How did that impact your relationship with yourself and loved ones?

Share out your reflections using #InspiringJY

AFFIRMATIONS

(Write, Draw, or Brainstorm ideas or thoughts here)

My educational story is...

Inspiring JOY invites us to examine how we can naturally and intentionally foster connections and infuse joy during our routine encounters with students. The strategies Jennifer shares are practical, manageable and **EMPOWERING**! This is the perfect resource to read as we prepare for our upcoming school year!
Suzanne Dailey, Instructional Coach & Host of the Teach Happier podcast

Lesson 15:
Dog Walk - House Rules

Today...I'm striving to be the person...my dog thinks I am.

 Launch:

Having a family dog is a lot of work! While they're incredibly cute, unfortunately, they don't arrive knowing how to do everything. There is a ton of intentional teaching involved when these fur babies join our lives. In our house, walking is a very important activity to our family. Our family uses regular walks for selfcare, exercise, and as a means to connect to each other and nature. Therefore, our four-legged friends must learn to walk with us from the very beginning.

If you've ever trained a dog, you understand that the first time you put a collar on a puppy, they scratch and wiggle to try and get it off. They have no interest in being confined and compliant. While eventually they can't imagine life without it; it definitely takes time, training, and patience from everyone.

After overcoming the collar challenge, the leash becomes a focus of attention. Once again they resist the initial idea of this even being introduced to their world. It's a struggle! Our puppies have always sat down and refused to move in the early training days. Sometimes, they would pull against the leash as we found ourselves in an excruciating game of tug a war. In fact, at some point every one of our puppies have pulled so hard that their tiny little heads would slip right out of the collar. For most puppies this is a process that can test our character as we wade through a sea of potentially frustrating attempts to manage behavior. I've found that putting the leash on them and letting them walk around the house without me even holding the leash helps them grow comfort and confidence for their new normal. Eventually, they let me very loosely pick up the leash in the house and very slowly we meander outside. But going outside with the leash attached was not at all like walking with the leash.

All 3 of my dogs initially hated the leash and didn't understand this annoying thing dangling near their face. They'd bite at it. They'd jump over it and get tangled. I remember times with them completely wrapping me up in the leash; where the only way out was for me to sit down to untangle myself. Needless to say puppy training can test us to our core.

I believe in three big rules that apply to all three of my dogs:

**All dogs would be on the leash at all times outdoors--Doing the right thing meant we were following state and local leash laws that would keep everyone safe.

**All dogs walk quietly with a bit of slack in the leash--Doing their very best on the walk allows them freedom to move around if their personality desires that but not pull so hard that someone might get hurt. Additionally, a quiet peaceful walk meant no barking or aggression that might agitate themselves or others.

**All dogs will stick to the path--Staying on a path helps us focus on others as we stay out of people's yards, avoid cars, bikes, and other dogs and people.

All 3 of my dogs have had strict "house rules" for walking that they were all expected to adhere to. On the other hand, each of my girls have had very different personalities and arrived with completely different past experiences. Therefore, I've built in freedom so we can learn the best practices for them on the leash.

Sammy was my very first dog. She was adorable, looked like a miniature lassie and had colors exactly the same. Sammy was adventurous and always pursuing things to eat. She was absolutely the biggest lap dog you have ever seen. As a dominant personality, she had a passion for looking around at anything and everything, while being the lead dog. When I was training her to walk on the leash, she was all over the place. She needed to sniff this and check out that. She was very curious about everything. It was chaos on a string. Additionally, she was a RUNNER, as she would take off in a heartbeat. My work with her centered around training Sammy to not only stay on the path, but I taught her that the entire path wasn't hers. Sharing is Caring! While she was an incredibly sweet girl, she lacked inherent empathy for others' space. She needed restrictions even within the sidewalk. However, I empowered her desire to lead by letting her walk right in front of me so that she could feel like she was in charge and protecting us all from danger.

Ginger was my sensitive dog. She had severe anxiety and was afraid of her own shadow. In fact, her anxiety story became the inspiration for a picture book I wrote called, ***I'm Who***, which helps children learn how to cope with their own overwhelming stress. She hated looking anyone in the eye and didn't really like people petting her or other dogs talking to her. She needed a routine and she needed to feel safe. Because Sammy was the toughest animal Ginger knew, they became instant best friends. She loved her sister Sammy and wanted to be with her at all times. At night, they would even sleep right next to each other. Adorable! With Sammy being a free spirit, I knew I needed a way to lead two dogs when I was walking them. Thus, I trained Ginger to walk on the left of Sammy, to ensure they could be next to each other. Capitalizing on Sammy's desire to lead and Ginger's loyotaly to her sister, helped ease Ginger's fear and Sammy's interest in running away. Ginger had a routine that she could understand. They both walked out in front of me with Ginger on the left and Sammy on the right. It was a perfect match for years! When Sammy eventually passed away Ginger still walked on the left; although, she began to walk directly next to me as she needed someone next to her.

Maya is my third baby dog. She's a super intuitive and sensitive dog. She has big eyes that love to look at and listen to all people and animals. She's particularly in tune with other's emotions. She bounced around at various homes before landing with us. When we got Maya, Sammy had already passed away and so we were left with only Ginger. Teaching Maya to walk on the right of Ginger gave Ginger comfort in a familiar roll as Sammy had been in. Unfortunately, that wasn't exactly what would work for Maya. Because of Maya's traumatic upheaval as a puppy, she has a bit of separation anxiety and is in constant fear of being abandoned. Maya's unique passion for bringing joy to others even led to me writing a picture book series, Award Winning Dog, to help teach SEL/character education to children around the world.

Award Winning Dog

Jennifer Appel

Illustrated by: Herb Leonhard

Maya is a dog that needs to be able to see everyone on the walk. If there are 3 people walking with her, she is constantly doing a headcount to make sure we are all there. Sometimes she would stop and look around to make sure we all are there if she can't see us. Being aware of her basic need for connection and reassurance, allowed me to modify my training and expectations. This modification forced me to locate a routine that perfectly positioned Maya to be able to see everyone on the walk. While the number of walkers made no difference to Sammy or Ginger, Maya needed to be able to interact with everyone. Thus, she had two positions that she walked in. When it was just the 3 of us, Ginger, Maya and Myself, Maya would walk in between Ginger and I to make sure she had full access to each of us.

When my husband joined in to make four of us, Maya would walk on my right and Ginger on my left. That way she could see me and my husband and look over to see Ginger. If other friends or family joined in, this 2nd routine worked well and we built in freedom for her to periodically do a quick headcount of everyone on the walk. For years, it was hilarious to watch how perfectly focused Ginger would walk, while Maya bounced around checking on each person in the walking party. Every once in a while, she would move over to be near Ginger to give her a kiss and then get back in line between me and my husband. After Ginger passed away, Maya continued this exact routine with anyone that walks with us.

Illustration by:
Herb Leonhard

Maya and Ginger

"Happiness is a warm puppy."
-Charles Schulz

Classroom teachers understand the need to fit routines, expectations, and accommodations to support all learners. As we learned in Award Winning Culture, House Rules apply to everyone within the school (or family) community.

How can we ensure that our house rules apply to each student? What safeguards might we build in to meet the legitimate needs of everyone? Are there guidelines for reaching the whole child within these overarching house rules? How are you ensuring that your house rules avoid cultural bias?

> ## Teachers with a Joyful mindset recognize individual differences while maintaining house rules that guide the entire school.

Meeting learners where they're at.

 Expectations: Educators will create a plan to support classroom needs, while still ensuring the execution of House Rules.

 Stuff: Application of House Rules to fit individual needs.

 Skills: Your house rules should focus on all 5 CASEL skills, self-awareness, self-management, social awareness, relationship skills, and responsible decision making.

Instruction/Activities:

Intentionally teaching the house rules is not just making a fun poster and hanging them up on the wall. There is time, work, and energy up front to teach students what each rule actually means; while also helping them understand how it looks for each individual. In the same way that I didn't buy a leash and expect my puppies to go for a 3 mile walk on day one, students also need time to interact with their new standards. Learners require consistency over weeks-months to teach, reintroduce, and reconstruct a new way of thinking and behaving.

A few years ago, I had a student who was extremely social, brillant, and sensitive; yet, had very little impulse control. Blurting answers out frequently, landed him in trouble in other classrooms. Ironically, his blurted out responses were often pretty insightful and I wanted a way for him to talk and touch base with others. Because his brain worked so quickly, writing a thought or question down was challenging. When something came to him, he needed to share it out or he'd forget it. Similar to Maya, this student needed constant peer check in time but could also become easily distracted by social endeavors if left entirely to his own devices.

The solution came from a flexible rolling desk where he could isolate himself away from others but then I intentionally built in time every 10 minutes for him to slide his desk over and join a group for discussion. While other teachers might have permanently isolated him or punished him when he got off track, or out of his seat to talk with a neighbor, an award winning classroom framework guided a new path forward. He respected the time of siloed individual work time because he knew there was a social break just around the corner. The predictability of that peer release time at regular intervals, allowed him to flourish in my room.

Additionally, we had an agreement that he could blurt out an on topic response if I paused during instruction. Thus, he wouldn't interrupt instruction but could share an answer so he felt included in the discussion. Many teachers would have scolded him for failing to 'do the right thing' or not 'do his best' because he was blurting out. But my willingness to understand his needs and recognize how his responses could positively impact everyone's learning compelled me to fit the house rules to this individual.

> House Rules are like a great instructional rubric--they're empowering-- they inform students what they CAN DO not just what they can't.

When teachers fail to recognize individual diversity they open themselves up to a form of discrimination that legal scholar Patricia Williams calls "spirit murdering." Bettina Love explains that "spirit murdering robs people of color of their humanity and dignity and leaves personal, psychological, and spiritual injury." This covert form of racism hurts the overall learning culture. Unfortunately, unintentional discrimination is not limited to ethnicity, but can span to sexual identity, religion, mental health, physcial and learning disabilities, gender, and more. House Rules must NEVER be a way to weaponize a classroom culture through social emotional learning.

"SEL is not a fancy way of having RULES at your school. It's not designed to oppress a marginalized group. It's quite literally a system for empowering others to live their best lives, with the necessary soft skills and character development that ensures thriving in an ever changing world." (Appel, 2020)

Occasionally, classroom behavior can flat out push our buttons. Students who sharpen pencils during direct instruction can be incredibly frustrating. One year, I remember a student getting up to sharpen their pencil in the middle of instruction because it had just become broken. At that moment, I knew she wasn't doing it because of defiance. Of course, it was still annoying as it coincided with the crescendo of the lesson. Rather than unleashing my irritation, I decided to pause and make this a culture teaching moment. As a group, we created a new class norm that if you have a 'pencil emergency' you would stand up and walk to the pencil sharpener and set your pencil in the sharpener and turn to look at me and wait. I would finish what I was in the middle of doing or saying. And then

I would pause and the student could sharpen their pencil and we could both get back to working. Choreographing student needs within instructional moments is an advanced form of pedagogical humility. You have to make adjustments when you see things come up in the moment, be flexible within the set rules.

How I intentionally teach House Rules at the beginning of the year.

Step 1: Frayer Model
- Have the students fill out the Frayer Model for each of the 3 house rules.
- Definition in their own words, what does it mean to them in a classroom/school setting.
- Create a sentence demonstrating students doing whatever the rule states, in my case it is answering the question.
- Give some examples of things they can do at school and in the classroom that exemplify this rule.
- Give some non-examples to show what might not be following this rule.
- Make sure that all of this is personal to them, what is their perspective and cultural lens about this idea or rule.

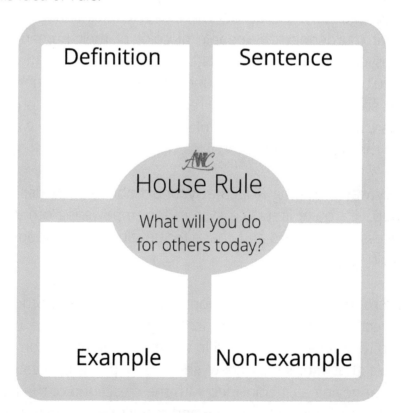

Frayer Model (Frayer, 2001)

(Frayer Model created by Dorothy Frayer at the University of Wisconsin in 2001: Example/Non-Example)

Step 2: District Policy

- We all have rules and routines that are required by your state or district and must be taught at the beginning of the year. I try to make it much more interactive and meaningful for the students instead of a lecture format. I have them relate the rules for the district back to the school house rules to understand the connection.
    - ○ Make copies of the district policies.
    - ○ Cut into strips with one rule/policy per strip.
    - ○ Match those with the House Rule.
        - ■ Students can place them in between or below to signal multiple House rules apply.

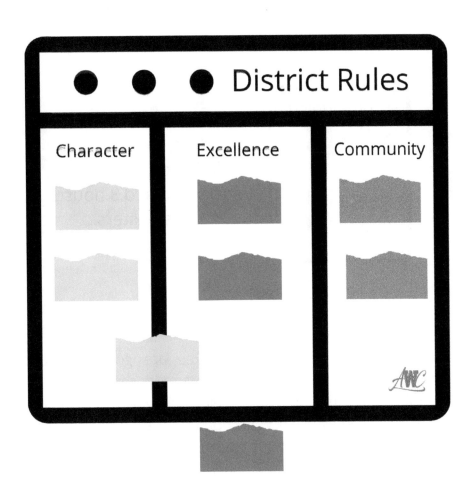

Step 3: Whole Class Brainstorm

- Create 3 large posters, one with each rule.
- Have the students look at all of the information they have put together about what the rules mean to them and how the district policies match each rule.
- Have them create one sticky note per rule that sums up all of the information and what it means to them. It could be in the form of a definition, ideas, examples, picture, or however they can describe it in that small space.
    - ○ Have them put their initials so you can see what each person thinks.

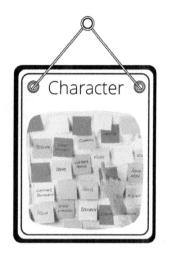

Students brainstorm ideas, examples, definitions and add sticky notes to 3 house rules posters.

 ## Close Intentionally:

Even with personalized rule definitions, mistakes are going to happen—and kids occasionally misbehave! Shocking, I know! Educators must seek out an established set of norms for each individual by remaining calm, seeing behavior as a communication of need, identifying strengths, and guide student reflection time. Learners can reimagine their own slip-ups when they reflect in terms of themselves and what they can do differently. When you have norms that are specific to learners every student is capable of abiding by the house rules.

 ## Opportunities:

Individual needs are important and we must adjust for each student. What it looks like for one, might be totally different for others. You also have to figure in prior knowledge based on their home environment and norms. That is why you have to come up with a definition for each of the 3 house rules for each individual person.

 **Needs:**

I relish when other teachers come to me and say, this student is being very successful in your class, what are you doing differently?

When you speak in a group parent meeting and the parent explains how their child is feeling successful in your classroom.

But most of all, when we see or hear about learners successfully using norms in other teacher's classrooms.

> WE CAN RECOGNIZE SUCCESS AT DIFFERENTIATING AND INDIVIDUALIZING HOUSE RULES WHEN STUDENTS GENERALIZE BEHAVIOR OUTSIDE OF OUR OWN SETTING.

 Self-Reflection:

What is your group definition of a house rule that everyone follows?

Describe a recent time you negatively reacted to a student based on what you thought "all" students should be doing?

How might you have used their strength to restructure problem behavior?

How can you use your own life lessons to guide discussions with students?

Share out your reflections using #InspiringJY

AFFIRMATIONS

(Write, Draw, or Brainstorm ideas or thoughts here)

HOUSE RULES HELP LEARNERS...

If you have invested your life in a career in teaching and learning, the first few pages of *Inspiring Joy* will do just that, and you won't be able to put it down. You will be captivated with every word that will **RESONATE DEEP** within you as you reflect on your own experience in the classroom, and the echoes of your own life with this newly illuminated path. When you get to the end of this book, you will be changed, with new ideas, a new sense of humility to rethink old ways, be challenged to raise your game--because you will know deep inside that you can do better, and just like the students you will inspire, you will do the same. **LIFE CHANGING BOOK**!
Andrea Samadi, Founder of Achieveit360.com and
Host of the Neuroscience Meets Social and Emotional Learning Podcast

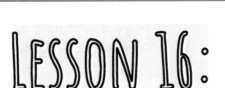

LESSON 16:

QUEEN FOR A DAY - AUTHENTIC BRANDING

And your 1995 homecoming queen is...

 **Launch:**

At Hanford High School, students didn't run for homecoming court, it was essentially a 'popularity' contest and on the initial voting people would just write in names of who they thought should win the award. For the first three years of my time in high school, the homecoming royalty was always for the rich, popular and pretty. To be honest with you, I really didn't think much of the homecoming queen. In movies and in my head they were always snobs that weren't very nice to other people. I had a preconceived notion of what it was supposed to be like to be a homecoming queen. Society had branded this position as something to be looked up to and that every girl should want to become. They also made it seem as though this was a position only for a certain 'type' of girl that looked down on others for not being up to a preferred status.

We all know that these stereotypes brought on by society are constantly reinforced in our media. Unfortunately, this specific branding of homecoming queen is not always positive. Thus, some people have created this misconception based on stereotypes that already exist.

When I was a senior in high school, I was one of the people in charge of homecoming, setting up the assembly, voting, and the dance. As an active member of our school's leadership, I was often at the forefront of creating these moments. When the initial voting results came in for the homecoming queen, I was beyond shocked to see my name on the list. I looked at all the other girls' names and thought--yeah, they fit. They should be nominated. They were all very popular and very pretty. Three of them had won freshman, sophomore, and junior princess, so their inclusion on our classes final top prize seemed completely warranted. I honestly didn't really think much about it since I was overwhelmed preparing for the assembly and the dance.

We had this tradition of selecting that year's queen and king in a special assembly. Nominees would sit at the bottom of the bleachers, while the previous year's king would walk up and down in front of all of the candidates, before finally stopping to dramatically reveal that year's queen. In an over the top type production, similar to ABC's The Bachelor, it was a mix of pomp and circumstance complete with a red rose.

Moments before the crowning, I had been running around frantically in charge of the assembly, when one of my friends asked me about sitting on the bench with the other nominees.

"Oh yeah...like I would win," I sarcastically responded with a hint of disdain for the entire affair.

But as a compliant kid, I snuck over and sat at the far end of the bench so as not to get in the way of the eventual selected queen. What happened in the next 2 minutes is quite honestly a bit of a blur. Apparently, the previous year's king walked all the way down, stopping in front of me. As he extended an arm out to me, I suddenly realized that I was anointed the homecoming queen. Standing up to thunderous applause, I really didn't know what to make of it all.

After the assembly, I was cleaning up and trying to get ready for the game, dance, and busy weekend ahead. A group of classmates came up to me and shared how happy they were that I was the homecoming queen. I expressed surprise, as I offered them up every opportunity to tell me it was a mistake. But this influential group reiterated to me:

"It isn't surprising--you are a great person, and that is who should represent our school and our class--You deserve to be honored--It should be someone that SERVES this school and is KIND to others."

> *"You too are a brand. Whether you know it or not. Whether you like it or not."*
> *-Marc Ecko*

I think if I'm being honest with myself, it probably took me several years to rebrand the role of homecoming queen in my own head. Over time, I learned that its portrayal on TV and movies was not fair to many incredible high school girls around the country (including me). My biggest takeaway from this inspiring honor was that our personal brand is what people say about us, when we're not around. Winning an honor I didn't even think I wanted taught me that the brand you choose to share with the world has a far reaching impact on others. My brand of kindness, empathy, and service allowed me to get along with many different social groups in high school.

Sharing our classroom brand is a critical way to connect with our school community...

> Teachers fostering an Award Winning Culture, intentionally craft an authentic brand within their individual classrooms.

Be purposeful about how you brand your classroom.

 Expectations: Setting up your classroom as a brand:
What do you want people to say about you as a teacher, your class and how it feels to be in your space?

 Stuff: A classroom filled with joyful leaders asking and answering the questions associated with Character, Excellence and Community.

 Skills: If you want to create a safe space for all of your students you want to make sure you think about all 5 CASEL skills: Self-awareness, self-management, social awareness, relationship skills, and responsible decision making.

 Instruction/Activities:

> *"I've learned that people will forget what you said, people will forget what you did, but people will never forget how you made them feel."*
> *-Maya Angelou*

Students won't remember every single piece of content that you taught. Many of our most sage advice, over the top projects, and stories teachers share will be lost over time. However, the feeling that learners experience in your care will unavoidably seep into the DNA of every kid you come in contact with; thus, impacting all the lives they'll touch for generations.

Studies have found that the average human being meets 80,000 people in their lifetime.

I can't help but assume this number might be even higher for teachers, who spend nearly 90,000 hours at school throughout their professional career. It's incredible to hypothesize all the influence that one teacher has to inspire joy.

Teachers have an awesome responsibility of NOT ONLY influencing the students who sit before us, but the ripple effect of future influenced relationships that each student carries with them. In our scientifically estimated 35,000 choices that we as humans make each day, it can be remarkable to imagine how a few intentional teaching decisions alter the life trajectory of our greater society's brand.

Mindful Moment

 Take a quiet minute to close your eyes and reflect back to a few of your most influential teachers you had growing up.

 Think about any and all of the incredible faces and names that popped through your head. Maybe it's your 2nd grade reading specialist, middle school science teacher, or the high school spanish teacher.

 What feelings come to mind as you intentionally reflect on these influential teachers? Better yet, how did these monumental feelings shape your personal brand?

What's the common thread that they all seem to possess? How has this thread impacted the classroom brand that you've tried to cultivate?

When setting up your classroom please take some time to reflect on all of the aspects you want your room to stand for. If your generic content is the only brand you're selling, your students may struggle to connect, learn, and ultimately remember their time with you.

In my classroom, I'm purposeful in the culture I'm striving toward. I want to evoke a feeling of safety, hope, and belief in themselves while teaching them to become a positive leader in their own lives. Our brand reveals our values; but, sometimes there are values that lie beneath our publicly acceptable and shared values that lurk below the surface. These "Shadow Values", as Jim Collins refers to them, are the deeper facets of our classroom that are the actual operating culture in learning spaces.

For example, one way to modify culture is through physical layout and furniture of the room. Before moving to flexible seating, I had two large bookshelf carts in the front of my room. It is where I had all the worksheets and supplies laid out for the day. Additionally, there was a huge stereo, and a bunch of 'stuff' on the shelf. It's amazing how often teacher 'stuff' invades student space!

My room always appeared to be highly organized and structured, while having that 'don't touch anything in the fancy living room' type experience. Thus, the shadow value that I wasn't even cognizant of was that students were expected to ask before taking something. This unofficial structure led to siloed learning rather than collaborative learning pods.

When I really began examining my brand, from a different angle, you could see that I was in the front of the room and I was being 'protected' by these two large carts. Unbenounced to me, I was blocking off the students from interacting with me. I had basically created this shadow value barrier in the front of my room to separate me from the learners. Was this how I wanted my students to feel about me? Unapproachable?

I want my students to feel that they are being heard, they're cared about, and encouraged to approach me anytime they need support. Thus, when I moved to flexible seating, I got rid of 95% of MY STUFF. Everything that survived the purge was put through the culture filter of: how is this item actually benefiting my students? I was literally transforming MY classroom, into THEIR learning hub. In OUR classroom, my desk was very small, in the front corner of the room, and the only item that was solely mine in the learning space. Everything in my room was set up for my students. [Side note: reimagining all items for learners rather than teachers built in student ownership that ironically strengthened student behavior and buy-in to take care of the room in ways that most teens might not even take care of their own bedroom].

There was no longer a front and back of the room. I had the traditional front where there was a projector and smartboard like every classroom that the district has decided for you. But I also had a TV set up on one side that was being projected to; thus, the students didn't have to all face the same direction. Wherever they sat, they were able to move about and see from anywhere in the room. The brand I started to convey was that you as the learner are far more important than things.

> *"We manage things but we lead people."*
> -James C Hunter

Nowadays, I never sit at my desk. I have a standing desk on wheels that I move around the room when necessary. But most of the time, I just grab my laptop and sit anywhere in the room with students. There is no more imaginary line between student and teacher. We're all learners! My kids feel my brand, from the moment they hit my doorway.

Every decision a teacher makes impacts the classroom culture. For example, teachers can invite cultural inclusion by having culturally diverse books on their bookshelf, rainbow safe space poster/sticker posted, using gender neutral pronouns, having materials available in multiple languages, and actively seeking student input on everything in the classroom. This is not meant to be an exhaustive list but more of a mindset.

Community Mindset welcomes a student oriented feeling of joy.

 ### Close Intentionally:

When you think about your classroom, what do you want people to see, hear, smell, feel in your edu-world?

Every action, choice, and expression will ultimately shape your brand.
What preconceived notion will learners and families have about your classroom?

Do you want people in the public to believe we are all like the boring economics teacher from Ferris Bueller droning on about "Voodoo Economics"?

Perhaps, you prefer to change the narrative and ensure the school community understands what your classroom is all about and how you're serving your learners.

 ### Opportunities:

Ironically, in our current state of education we have to intentionally teach learners things like choice, voice, and agency. The system itself has literally trained the student autonomy right out of our most important stakeholders. If you have students that are having a hard time with flexible seating, have them test out different areas of the room and see what works best for them. The most successful learners experiment with different settings, styles, and approaches to their metacognition. Students might need to have headphones and listen to music to help them concentrate. They may benefit from some extra help and thus enjoy sitting near you, within the classroom. Perhaps, they thrive off movement; therefore, you must prearrange to have them bounce between locations depending on the task.

For virtual learning, here is a fun visual I used with my kids for Zoom breakout rooms. This was a great way to meet individual needs even remotely.

Breakout Room Options

Wildcat Room	Community Room	Character Room	Excellence Room

Stay with the teacher and ask a question.	Discussion, Camera on and talking to classmates.	Quiet Discussion, camera on or off, muted, and talking in the chat.	Quiet work time, turn off camera and mute.

Teachers crafting a successful brand challenge their learners to actively search and discover how THEY learn best!

 ### Needs:

One time, a group of puzzled girls sat down on the floor, in the "front" of my room discussing something. Walking over to the inquisitive group, I asked them if they needed help. One of the girls looked up from their sidebar and questioned:

"Why is your room so much bigger than our other classrooms? I thought they were all the same, but yours is way bigger? Why?"

I broke it to them that it actually wasn't any larger. Instead, I had chosen to get rid of all of my personal stuff to create more space for students. Another girl piped in:

"Well, I guess that's why your room feels so much different than the other classes, it is kinda all about us in here--isn't it?"

As we spoke about some of the specifics on how my room felt different from their other classrooms, I realized that these girls were feeling the exact brand I was desperate to create for all my learners.

Do large groups of students come hang out in your room before or after school? Do former students make a point of coming and visiting your classroom? Are students and parents frequently requesting that their student has YOU as a teacher? Chances are...your authentic brand is being recognized by others!

 **Self-Reflection:**

What do students think about your classroom?

Do you have an emotional or metaphoric "wall" up in your room?

What personal misconceptions do you have that you can repurpose into becoming a life lesson for your learners?

Share out your reflections using #InspiringJY

AFFIRMATIONS

(Write, Draw, or Brainstorm ideas or thoughts here)

MY BRAND SOUNDS LIKE...

Inspiring JOY takes us on an adventure of **REDISCOVERY** and **AWAKENING** to not only be better educators, but to ultimately provide students with a profound experience of learning, connecting, & building relationships that last...and ultimately, **inspiring JOY**!

Traci Browder, M.Ed., Intelligogy, LLC, Betterflies, Grit-CrewEDU Co-Founder

LESSON 17:
ANGRY ELF-PERSONAL OUTREACH

🚀 Launch:

Observing my dad flourish as an elementary principal was such a lucky childhood gift. He believed very strongly in supporting his students outside of the classroom by spending time with them when they were having fun and playing outside at recess. Rather than viewing it as supervision, he saw this time as an intentional way to foster character, SEL, and community through kickball, football games, and fly-fishing instruction. From an early age, I learned the value in educators meeting students where they were.

As a middle school teacher, with no recess to speak of, I've always made a concentrated effort to be in the hallway before school, after school, and at all of the passing times. Choosing hallway time over emails or last minute lesson planning, helped open me up to real connection, support and culture building with my students. Greeting students at the doorway or locker allowed me to look into the eyes of everyone I'd be hoping to inspire that day. This pre-set personal outreach helped me prevent many behavioral disasters from crossing into instruction.

One year, I had a student that would arrive at school every day at 7:20am, even though we didn't start until 8. He'd invariably make a direct beeline to his locker, grabbing his stuff and then head straight to my class for the first period. I noticed from the first day of school he was going to be someone that needed extra love and attention. This angry little elf would storm in my class tightly clutching his binder to his chest; sometimes, I was sure he might snap his binder in half. His face had hardened lines and a permanent frown of a much older jaded young man. Like a trapped animal needing to break loose from shackles of whatever life had thrown his way--he was hurting!!

I remember going to the counselor and asking about the history of this obviously traumatized student. Apparently, he had a history of violence, aggression, and fights at his previous school. After learning some background, I decided the proactive strategy for supporting him was to encourage him to come into my room each day to relax in a safe, quiet space before starting his school day.

During class he was a great student. He did all of his work, but was eerily quiet as his anger seemed to be seething underneath the surface like an active volcano ready to erupt. Eventually after about a week, I started to talk with him a little... but only after he was able to cool down for a few minutes. I told him he was welcome to grab a snack, listen to music, whatever he needed. For a few weeks he would just look at me and not really say anything. I never pushed. Instead, I simply extended that well placed olive branch of patient outreach each day he arrived early to my room.

Over the course of the year, he slowly got to the point of telling me what had happened each day. Some days he had a lot of violence in his home. He was frequently woken up to hear a fight his father was having with someone in the house that involved intense rage. Each morning, he came to school desperately trying to cope with his frustrations the only way he knew how.

Afterall, we all do the best we can to survive.

It's hard to put into words how rewarding it was to watch him lessen his grip on that binder each morning. I was so proud to see him slowly interacting with his peers as he removed his self imposed emotional wall preventing more pain. He started taking down all of the chairs, helping set up the room, and just generally doing anything he could do to make himself useful before school. He was always eager to jump up and hand papers out or deliver supplies to table groups. He'd instruct other students what supplies they needed for the day. I was witnessing the power of him transforming into a kid who was driven to serve others.

As Hans reminds us, *"Greeting is the Gateway to Belonging."* Two years later, he eventually became my outstanding 8th grade teacher's assistant. He loved supporting younger students, as he taught, shared great ideas, and was surprisingly patient with my most challenging learners. Watching him bounce around my room, like a seasoned teacher one could never have imagined how this young man would lead a culture fostering human connection. From angry and isolated to friendly leader--his metamorphosis was complete.

INTENTIONALLY GREETING OUR STUDENTS EACH DAY, PROVIDES TEACHERS A CHANCE TO LEARN THE REAL SECRETS OF REACHING OUR MOST CHALLENGING KIDDOS.

Understanding your students on another level.

 <u>**Expectations:**</u> Warmly greet your students and welcome them to the classroom everyday. Do a quick evaluation of their state of mind and readiness to learn as they walk into the classroom.

 <u>**Stuff:**</u> Greeting your classes at the door is more important than sending an email or checking your grades, or various other administrative tasks.

 <u>**Skills:**</u> When we are intentional about greeting students we are helping them practice relationship skills and become socially aware.

 <u>**Instruction/Activities:**</u>

Myth: Passing time, recess, before or after school---that is ALL MY TIME to work. It's not student time!

Truth: While it's important to build in consistent personal moments of "breaks, balance, and boundaries" (Evan Whitehead), school time is STUDENT TIME. They need us to engage, connect, and reach out to help support them during non-instructional times.

Let me be clear...anytime you are at school is kid time. A teacher in an "Award Winning Culture values PEOPLE over paperwork" (Appel, 2020). You can do paperwork anytime, kids are what matter most. Give yourself grace and understanding in finishing up grading, emails, and planning as you lean into those personal outreach opportunities. Spending 5 minutes to greet students at the door, will save even more instructional time during the day.

> *"What's predictable is preventable."*
> -Dr. Robert Anda

If we can anticipate what a student is feeling when they enter our room we can offer strategic support, avoid mistakes impeding learning, and foster student/teacher relationships.

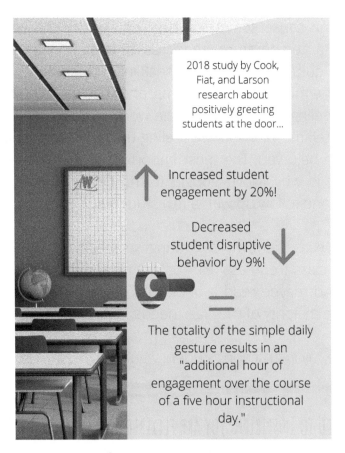

2018 study by Cook, Fiat, and Larson research about positively greeting students at the door...

↑ Increased student engagement by 20%!

Decreased student disruptive behavior by 9%! ↓

= The totality of the simple daily gesture results in an "additional hour of engagement over the course of a five hour instructional day."

When I see a student that is suffering or just having a bad day, I always ask them during the entry task if they need to talk or let me know if they are in need of anything. That is usually all they need: I SEE YOU. Teacher's acknowledgement of student feelings allows students to transition into learners. Other times they really do need to talk and I take them out in the hall and we talk for a minute before deciding our next steps from there (set a follow up appointment, connect with other school support staff, or personalize a plan for class time today). Sometimes it is serious enough for them to go see the counselor; while, other times they just need a minute to process their thoughts or write in their journal to express how they are feeling.

Students often are in need of something that they are not getting, like sleep, food or love. "Maslow before Bloom" (Pearlman, 2020), reminds me to encourage learners to go and get a snack from the cabinet, go to one of the comfy chairs and relax for a little while, or sit quietly listening to some music so they can get back to work and focus. By giving them that small moment to let me know how they are feeling they are able to be much more productive. Some teachers think this is a waste of time and demand that their students need to start working immediately. This short-sided view on valuing work production over a student's health and wellbeing will rarely work out. By giving them that 5-10 minutes they need, they are able to work for the other 45-50 minutes. If I don't get them what they need, they won't do anything for 60 minutes. 45 minutes of focused learning is far superior to 60 minutes of dis-engaged learning.

There are times that I can sense something is going on with the whole class so that is when I will give them a temperature check as a class to see what is happening. Temperature checks are quick mental health check-ins with students to see how they are feeling. I have always done mine on google forms, and they have 3 simple questions. One is to rate how they are feeling 1-5. One being the worst, 5 being the best. Number 2 asks them, would you like to tell me why you are feeling that way. And then number 3 is what do you need from me to help you. The most important aspect of this is that you look at them immediately. That is why I love google forms because I can very quickly get a snapshot of the feelings and follow up with a few students.

Additionally, I will share with them my self-rating so that they know what I am feeling. Sometimes I'll share the class trend as well. For example, if the whole class is a 2, we will just change the plans and maybe read a book that day, or do some journaling. We are able to adjust to what the majority of the class needs.

Pacing charts don't guide my instruction. Students' guide my instruction.

> TEACHERS COMMITTED TO INSPIRING JOY ARE FLEXIBLE AND CREATIVE IN THEIR ABILITY TO PIVOT LESSON PLANS TO FIT STUDENTS' NEEDS.

 ## Close Intentionally:

Not all students will say hi, or even acknowledge you as they walk in. They may try to ignore you or look away because they don't trust the relationship yet. This is 100% okay. You are there to extend the olive branch (or high five) to them. If they don't respond, don't be offended, it is NOT ABOUT YOU! Rather than demanding student engagement upon greeting, demand empathy and patience of the process from yourself. Connecting with our most challenging students takes time, trust, and tenacity! You are there for them and they eventually understand you will be there for them no matter what. Trust the process.

 ## Opportunities:

Elementary - try to greet your kids everyday in the morning when they are lined up outside and the same for after recess, greet them and see how they are feeling after being outside running around. Recess is like a whole different world. I see lots of elementary teachers even have a sign that kids can hit on the way in saying how they are feeling. You can do a special handshake with them on the way in as well. Better yet--

spend one recess per week outside with your students. You'll be amazed to see all the interpersonal dynamics of the playground. Plus, it's a great way to connect outside of content. If they see you having fun and playing outside everyone enjoys a new school perspective and relationship connection.

High School - They are never too old to be greeted at the door. They love to see you just as much, even if they don't always express it. Express genuine interest in how they are feeling that day. High school is extremely stressful so understanding their current state of mind is vital. Beyond greeting before class, high school kids love having teachers show up at their sports, activities, and events. Observing, cheering or participating in student's nonacademic passions build bridges into student learning back in the classroom.

 ## Needs:

While teachers have INCREDIBLE BLADDER CONTROL--Every once in a while I have to use the restroom in between classes. I recognize the success of greeting kids at the door, when I return from the bathroom with a standing line of kids waiting for me at my door. They love personal outreach so much that they'll literally stand there and wait before entering our room. They are waiting to say hi and don't want to go in until I am there to greet them. Occasionally, they'll even question other teachers "is Mrs. Appel sick," if I'm not lined up ready to say hi.

 ## Self-Reflection:

How are you intentionally greeting your students?

How are you reacting, relating and supporting regulation of emotions to help each learner have a positive day?

Think of an at-risk student who you slowly reached. How did you connect with that kiddo and how might you apply those life lessons to other learners?

AFFIRMATIONS
(Write, Draw, or Brainstorm ideas or thoughts here)

I USE PERSONAL OUTREACH TO...

I **LOVE** this book! Jennifer really brings it! A glorious, colorful romp with a close look at classroom branding and intentionality. Hat, cell phones, no problem. Lesson design stressing character & Project Based Learning, all set. Empowering kids through voice and choice, right here. Morning meetings with purpose, flexible seating, SEL, trauma informed teaching, got it. A thoroughly **DELIGHTFUL** book filled with joyous stories of growth and transformation, character building, academic excellence and inspiration on every page. This one!

Mrs. Rita M. Wirtz, MA, Author/Blogger

LESSON 18:

EMPATHY THRU TRAGEDY-EXPERIENCE

 **Launch:**

> *"Some of life's best lessons are learned at the worst times."*
> *-Ani DiFranco*

Receiving a call at 11:30 p.m, a few days after Christmas was a startling moment. As a 20 something year old teacher, with an established bed time of a seasoned morning person; close family and friends knew you'd never reach me after 9p.m. But for some odd reason, I found myself up well past my bedtime as if my body was preparing me for an incoming tragedy.

I picked up the phone and was instantly surprised by my aunt's frantic voice. Apparently, my dad's sister had been trying to get a hold of my father with no success. In a time that predated smartphones, my parents had traveled down to Florida to spend Christmas with my brother. Thus, she had no way of getting through to them, as this was a time when people generally shut off their cell phone at night. [I know...I've completely confused my younger readers. You'll have to trust me: phones didn't use to be appendages!] Naturally, I told her I'd be glad to relay a message and have dad contact her as soon as possible. I could feel the sense of intensity and urgency in her plea to reach my dad but I had no forewarning for what I was about to hear...

"Well, we need your dad because our parents were killed in a car crash today." Her words burned right through my senses. "He is the oldest and needs to help us," she shared in a desperate numb tone.

I was stunned at first; but quickly realized that I needed to spring into action. When met with emotional adversity, social scientists explain that we have the capacity to experience a duality of feelings AND thoughts. Dr Susan David says we can "helicopter above our

169

emotions" when we use internal dialogue such as: 'I notice myself feeling angry or sad.' This "metaview" of our emotional experience allows a psychological pause to make a choice moving forward. Ultimately, this moment of choice allows us to answer a character defining question: 'Who do I want to be in this moment?'

Pushing my own emotions into this reflective pause, I focused on teasing out the details so that I'd be prepared to inform my dad of this tragedy. According to my aunt, her sister, son, and my grandparents had all been together following church heading to a nice family brunch while my aunt drove the car. Meanwhile, the roads were really icy and a truck going in the opposite direction on the freeway was going full speed. The driver, failing to account for the icy roads, lost control before swerving across the median towards our family's car. My aunt tried to swerve to avoid the truck coming straight at them, but the roads were awful and she didn't have a lot of time or control. Unfortunately, the truck slammed into the side of her car with my grandparents both taking the brunt of the impact on their side.

As a trauma nurse, my aunt had tried to perform CPR, but realized it was too late for both my grandparents; they died within minutes after the crash. In addition to losing my grandparents, my aunt and cousin had also gone through an extremely traumatic experience. Hanging up with my aunt, I turned my attention to placing the hardest phone call I'd ever made in my life.

Reaching out to my brother at nearly 3am and asking him to wake up our father to come to the phone was an experience in extreme empathy, and I wouldn't wish it on anyone. Somehow I found the strength to put some coherent thoughts together to break this heart wrenching news to dad. Frankly, I don't remember my own exact words that night. However, I am crystal clear on how my intentional effort to focus on my dad's needs helped support him through a challenging personal experience.

I lost my grandparents, but my dad lost his parents and needed to be able to process this information and understand from me what had happened. I told my dad about his parents, what his sisters needed from him, and that they were eagerly awaiting their big brother's support. While it was one of the most difficult conversations I have ever had to have, I distinctly remember thinking that it was not about me today...I needed to be strong to support my dad. He was the person that mattered in this moment. There would be time for my own grieving soon, but that day I was driven to make his experience as supportive as humanly possible.

We can lift other's experience by focusing on their needs during trying times. These forms of kindness, service, and empathy create lasting memories of positivity.

> Teachers who inspire JOY believe that every child deserves to have an awesome classroom experience despite whatever's going on in the world.

I couldn't undue my grandparents death; in the same way that teachers can't wish away adverse childhood experiences at home. We don't control the world our learners live in outside of school. But from 8 am-3 p.m each day, we can actively fight for an award winning experience in our classrooms.

Thinking about others' experiences.

 Expectations: Elevating community members' experience as they enter our classrooms. We want them to feel welcome and valued.

 Stuff: Use empathy as a core to lifting others' experiences.

 Skills: When we create these amazing experiences for guests students become acutely aware of how to build relationships.

 Instruction/Activities:

> *"We rise by lifting others up."*
> *-Robert Ingesoll*

Traditional teachers instruct their students to ignore guests when they come in for a classroom observation. Obviously, the goal being for learners to stay focused on the content. But there's a better way. Every observation is an opportunity to practice real life 'soft skills' like making eye contact, saying hello, shaking hands, and generally making each guest feel special.

When we have a supervisor, colleague, or other community member come into our room, I relish the chance to make their day a little better. And even more importantly, how might we prepare and teach our students to make each person feel important? Do we view the outsider as a guest or an observer? The distinction matters in our effort to elevate their experience to the next-level.

Consider the language difference between OBSERVER and GUEST. The former implies a removed onlooker relegated to the cheap seats. While the latter implies a welcomeness that might feel like a warm chocolate chip cookie upon entry.

OBSERVER vs. GUEST

OBSERVER	GUEST
Passive	Active
Siloed	Community
Careful	Cared For
Forgotten	Memorable
Guarded	Engaging
Staged	Authentic

Put yourself in their shoes. If you're checking out a fellow teachers' classroom, do you hope to be viewed as an observer or guest?

When my grandparents died, all I could think about was how my dad felt. I didn't want to make the situation worse than it already was. When someone enters your classroom you want to focus on creating such a spectacular experience that whatever happened before they arrived melts away as they instantly understand they belong! They deserve to feel the same way that your students do: seen, valued, and loved.

When I have district officials or others come into my classroom I always try to have something for them to write on if they don't have anything. Frequently, I have sticky notes or note cards, so they can leave a positive note for my students. They can observe them and see what they are doing that is great and leave a note for them. Incidentally, this form of modeling will pay strong dividends as I'm actually intentionally teaching uninformed guests how to lead with kindness in other classrooms they might visit in the future.

When I have community members visit my classroom, I always hit on a couple key points.

- First, I always let them know where the best place to park is and how they can check in at the office.

- Second, I let ALL of the office staff know who is coming to see my students. Upon arrival at the front entrance, they can be greeted by name and ushered down to the correct location. [It seems like such a little thing but these little details add up to big feelings of positivity.]
- If they are arriving at a specific time, I have a student run down to the office to meet and greet them; before welcoming them down to our classroom.
  - Plus, I always ask ahead of time if they will need anything specific for their visit so that we can have everything ready for them.
- Next, I make sure that my class has a small handmade gift to give them as they leave to thank them for their visit and taking time out of their day to come and see our classroom (handmade card with the school logo, sticker, candy, gift card, etc.).
- Lastly, I always have the students write a handwritten thank you note afterwards to specifically thank them for what they provided us (time, energy, attention).

 ## Close Intentionally:

Before hosting a guest, new student, or other person in your classroom, visualize how you might be intentional to create a memorable experience. Many times, outsiders are ignored in the classroom. Will your class provide a unique greeting? Will they have a special seat in the room? How might they interact with students? Can you hang information, QR code or signage that helps them acclimate to today's learning target?

 ## Opportunities:

Now, to turn this around, if I ever observe other classrooms, I always write a handwritten note and leave it on the teachers desk thanking them for letting me come in and observe. I want to emphasize at least one awesome thing I enjoyed during my visit. Opening our door to colleagues can feel like a slippery slope to inviting open criticism or judgement. It's imperative to remember the professional risk that someone else took, when you're privileged enough to check out the work of your peers.

Sometimes the guest is not an adult at all. How you treat a new student is even more important than a fellow educator. Do you roll out the red carpet for a new learner or do you passively let them slink into a desk near the back? Most students will decide what they think about you and their chances to be successful in your room in the first 30 seconds of walking in the door. Will your learners offer to show them around? Will they discover a personalized treat upon their arrival to class? Will you intentionally compliment them or spread positivity on Day #1? Being the new kid in a classroom is incredibly overwhelming. How will you facilitate their transition socially to a new group of peers?

 **Needs:**

Next time your principal observes your classroom, encourage them to include students into their process.

Students can:
-answer questions for the principal
-share what they are learning
-talk about how they are feeling in the class
-provide feedback about curriculum, content, and class community

> LET'S HELP OTHERS PIVOT FROM WATCHING, EXAMINING, AND MONITORING TOWARD AN EXPERIENCE FILLED WITH INVOLVEMENT, INCLUSION, AND INSPIRATION.

 Self-Reflection:

When you have a guest in your room, take a moment to think about one quick question: how might they feel in your classroom?

Do you have something for people that enter your space? (Maybe it's a tangible treat, warm smile followed by a high five, or a class ritual of everyone turning and waving at the guest in unison)

Do you have students write thank you notes for guests that take time to come into your classroom? Could they take 30 seconds to do something similar for a new student on a post-it-note?

Think of a time that someone sincerely elevated your experience. Maybe it was an act of generosity, customer service, or love. How might you recreate that feeling for others in your care?

Share out your reflections using

AFFIRMATIONS

(Write, Draw, or Brainstorm ideas or thoughts here)

I will leave all who enter my classroom with an experience Rich in...

Inspiring Joy takes the reader on a journey through reflections, relevant quotes, storytelling, and life lessons. Jennifer Appel demonstrates the way in each chapter by expanding on the **LESSICONS** template infusing social-emotional learning, character development, and your WHY into the curriculum to personalize any assignment with opportunities to empower student motivation, confidence, and self-discovery. This book is a **MUST-READ** for educators who want to live a more joyful existence by practicing authenticity in the classroom that inspires and unlocks sustainable **JOY** in their learners.

Barbara Bray, Creative Learning Strategist, Podcast Host, Speaker, Keynoter, Author of Define Your Why

COMMUNITY LESSON PLAN

 LAUNCH:

WHY DO WE NEED TO THINK ABOUT OTHERS? WHY DO YOU THINK SOMETIMES IT IS GOOD TO WRITE SOMETHING OUT ON PAPER INSTEAD OF JUST TYPING, TEXTING OR SAYING?

 EXPECTATIONS:

- STUDENTS WILL LEARN HOW TO WRITE A PROPER THANK YOU NOTE TO EXPRESS GRATITUDE.
- STUDENTS WILL LEARN HOW TO PERSONALIZE EXPERIENCE THROUGH CARD WRITING.

 STUFF:

- THANK YOU CARDS OR PAPER
- PEN OR PENCIL

SKILLS:

STUDENTS WILL LEARN SOCIAL AWARENESS AND RELATIONSHIP SKILLS.

INSTRUCTION/ACTIVITES:

- TEACHER NOTE: THE PURPOSE OF THIS ACTIVITY IS TO TEACH STUDENTS ABOUT THE IMPORTANCE OF WRITING OR RECEIVING PERSONALIZED LETTERS OR CARDS BY HAND.
    - STUDENTS WILL LEARN TO APPRECIATE THE IMPACT OF A HANDWRITTEN CARD AND HOW TO PERSONALIZE THAT FOR EACH INDIVIDUAL.
- EXPLAIN THE MEANING OF GRATITUDE [AN OVERWHELMING APPRECIATION OR THANKFULNESS].
    - THE SCIENCE OF GRATITUDE SUGGESTS THAT HUMANS WHO PRACTICE GRATITUDE HAVE FEWER TOXIC EMOTIONS AND MENTAL HEALTH STRUGGLES, IMPROVED BRAIN CHEMISTRY, AND BECOME WIRED FOR JOY.

Inspiring Joy

- You will give the students either pre-made thank you cards, or you can easily have them fold a piece of paper to make a card.
- They need to choose someone to write a note to that they are grateful for right now in their lives. This is not an activity to do on Mother's Day or Grandparents Day, no special occasion. Be intentional about not just selecting a stereotypical holiday. This ensures that students are given free choice to choose ANYONE that is important to them.
  - Teacher Note: Emphasize empathy here. Have the students imagine what they would like to read in a letter to themselves and then project that to the person they are writing to.
  - Have students visualize the person and think about their character, personality, identity, uniqueness, and how they have impacted them.
- When you have them write the card - they need to format it correctly, always have them put the name at the top and then the writing in a paragraph underneath. They will then sign their name at the bottom with a salutation (love, a heart, sincerely, thank you, smiley face, etc.).
  - You will be surprised how many students have never written a card and don't know the proper format.
- I explain to them what a VIP is, a Very Interesting Person. They are who you are writing the card to and you want them to feel special and that you are paying attention.
- When you are writing the card you want to give specifics about the person and why they mean so much to you. It's critical to encourage students to be specific and give positive details about the VIP.
- Have the students put the card in an envelope and address (this has to be intentionally taught, again surprised at how many have never sent something in the mail).
- If they are not where the student can drop off the card to them in person, see if you or their parents can mail it to the recipient.

 ## CLOSE INTENTIONALLY:

- Discussion:
  - Think about how you would feel getting a note that was handwritten from someone, how is that different than a text message. You feel like they took the time to write you something specific.
  - Why should others be treated like a VIP, deserving of a wonderful handwritten note?

 ## OPPORTUNITIES:

- For elementary school, you can have the students write a shorter card depending on age level, they may just have a sentence that is written with a cute drawing.
- For high school you can have them do the exact same activity, they are old enough to maybe even write a letter instead of just a card.
- Another additional idea is to have the students write a positive letter to themselves that you would then mail to them when they are seniors in high school ready to graduate. I do this with my 6th graders and look up the HS they are attending and send them to the schools to give to the students. If the student moves away, they always send me an email asking me to send their letters. They love this activity.
- Another idea is to write a letter to each student at the end of the year. This is a great way to model positive letter writing to your students while also providing them with a meaningful keepsake. I do this on a paper yearbook that I hand out to students during the last week of school, with photos from the year. I also have a digital version that I have done for them and I type their letter and then sign it.
- During conferences and open house, I have guardians write personal notes to their child. Then, I intentionally hand these out when I notice a student needing a boost, during the school year.

 NEEDS:

- THE BEST ASSESSMENT FOR THIS ACTIVITY IS THE POSITIVE RESPONSE FROM THE RECIPIENTS OF THE HANDWRITTEN CARDS. THE MOST INFLUENTIAL EVIDENCE IS WHEN THE STUDENT RECEIVES ONE BACK FROM SOMEONE OR WHEN A STUDENT OPTS TO WRITE A HEARTFELT NOTE, ON THEIR OWN MONTHS LATER. I'VE EVEN RECEIVED NOTES FROM STUDENTS YEARS LATER, WHO WERE IMPACTED BY ME. THESE ARE THE MOST SPECIAL FORMS OF PAY-IT-FORWARD GRATITUDE THAT A TEACHER CAN RECEIVE.
- FAMILY CONNECTION: ONE OF THE WAYS TO CONTINUE THE WORK OF BUILDING COMMUNITY IS TO INVOLVE FAMILIES IN THE PROCESS. HERE IS AN EXAMPLE POST THAT YOU COULD PRINT AND SEND HOME WITH KIDS, POST ON SOCIAL MEDIA AND YOUR LEARNING MANAGEMENT SYSTEM, OR SEND IN AN EMAIL.

COMMUNITY

WHAT WILL YOU DO FOR OTHERS TODAY?

> In class today, we did an activity to teach about showing gratitude for others, thank you card writing, and why personalization is important.
>
> Here are some reflection questions for you to discuss as a family:
>
> - What situations in our family call for a handwritten thank you card?
> - What are we doing for others today?
> - What is an activity that we can do as a family to serve others?

 SELF-REFLECTION:

- REFLECT ABOUT YOUR CLASS:
  - DID YOU HAVE ANYONE RESIST THE IDEA?
  - DID YOU HAVE ANYONE THAT WASN'T SURE WHAT TO WRITE, THAT WAS REFUSING TO DO THE ACTIVITY?
    - STUDENTS THAT ARE RESISTANT TO THIS PROBABLY HAVE NEVER RECEIVED A HANDWRITTEN NOTE BEFORE, SEND THEM A CARD AFTER THIS ACTIVITY. THEY NEED TO SEE WHAT IT FEELS LIKE TO RECEIVE HANDWRITTEN LOVE.
- EXTENSION: ONCE STUDENTS ARE TAUGHT THIS SKILL, THEY APPLY THIS IN OTHER SITUATIONS. THEY WRITE THANK-YOUS TO COMMUNITY MEMBERS, VOLUNTEERS, TEACHERS, STAFF, OTHER STUDENTS, ANYONE THAT IS IMPACTING OUR SCHOOL.

Conclusion

"The best time to plant a tree was 20 years ago.
The second best time is NOW."

-Chinese Proverb

A few years ago, when starting our PBIS program, I began planting award winning seeds all over my 6th grade classrooms. The idea being, as they grew into 7th and 8th grade young leaders, they might eventually be able to help stretch their character in ways that fostered an excellent community for our entire school.

I was committed to teaching students to participate and eventually run our school store. Because the store was going to be open during lunch time, I knew that I'd have to trust my students to lead the work while I was teaching class at that time. When looking for a couple of 8th graders I thought would be perfect for this task, I reflected upon students who demonstrated a passion for servant leadership. It wasn't about finding overpowering students to boss younger 6th graders around. I was looking for students who actively worked on their own character (humility, patience, kindness, empathy, etc.) I needed mentally strong leaders.

Conclusion

The two students I chose had been rockstar students in my class in 6th grade. They were the perfect fit for the job and were amazing TA's and took total ownership over the store, customer experience, and helping my younger students. Those two young ladies ran with the responsibility in so many possible ways. They were empowered to decorate and organize the store however they desired; while being accountable to each other. They were given full autonomy but asked to demonstrate total character at all times. It was a trust based relationship. It became THEIR shop and they took immense pride and proprietorship over this little school activity. The first half of the year was smooth sailing...

During the third quarter, a group of younger leaders had been having a few interpersonal issues during lunch that led to some negative reports of inappropriate behavior to me. When I asked my two trusted TA's about it, they told me that they wanted to take care of it. While I appreciated their initiative, I couldn't help but wonder if this would eventually land back in my adult lap to fix...

> WHEN WE TRULY HOPE TO INVEST IN BUILDING UP OTHERS, IT'S CRITICAL TO PROVIDE SUPPORT, RESOURCES, AND GUIDANCE, WITHOUT ELECTING TO TAKE OVER.

The next day, my 8th grade TA's announced that they planned to close the shop to the rest of our student body because they felt that THEY hadn't done a good job training the group of young leaders. Imagine the level of insight and accountability that it takes for a teenager to own other student's misbehavior. They believed that they needed to work with the younger students more before we were able to open again successfully.

Think about the maturity, humility and emotional agility it requires to accept personal responsibility in the ones we teach rather than blaming our learners for their negative behavior. The lessons that I taught them in the past informed the choices they made as 8th graders when impacting those younger students.

"If your actions create a legacy that inspires others to dream more, learn more, do more and become more, then, you are an excellent leader."
-Dolly Parton

After receiving the okay from me, my student leaders facilitated a group meeting in the shop with team building activities focused on bonding to increase morale and connection amongst each other. The TA's had taken it upon themselves to research and create a fully

180

developed project based plan with experiential activities to promote cohesion and a character-focused school store culture.

These remarkable young leaders understood that leadership is influence--plain and simple. Choosing NOT to lecture or simply talk at others was strong evidence at how powerful activities can promote an inspiring organizational culture. This school store team needed to be united and have fun together. These activities earned them respect and influence, which ultimately led to authority. The rest of the quarter went off without a hitch. The group worked great together and received glowing endorsements from students and staff on their professionalism and PBIS purpose. These two leaders had reached a special level of personal development as they modeled these critical soft skills for their younger teammates.

Please understand--academic aptitude and content understanding are not the end goals for our work. If I'm being honest, I could care less about test scores, grades, or a regurgitation of mandated benchmarks.

The goal of school is to deeply connect learning while applying it to passion. This purpose filled form of education puts teachers and students in the role of joy inspirers.

I want my kids to THINK--DREAM--LOVE! I want to raise an army of great human beings driven to make the world a better place--even when Mrs. Appel is no longer around...

It's amazing to witness our tiny seeds of legacy starting to become fully rooted JOY POWERED LEARNING LEADERS. It's remarkable what empowered learners can do, create, and become...

"Teachers have the gift to GIVE."
-Livia Chan

You are an amazing teacher. You're planting your own educational seeds to take our classrooms, schools and communities to the next level. I know first hand how difficult it is to be an educator. YOU MATTER! THIS WORK MATTERS! I know it can feel like a real grind. It's hard work---THANK YOU!!!

I urge you to locate those other educators (in person or virtually) driven to inspire JOY...turning to them for mutual support, connection and inspiration.

And I'm thrilled to be your cheerleader on your continual quest to support student JOY.

"You can't go back and change the beginning,
but you can start where you are and change the ending."
-C.S. Lewis

Reflect on your own life stories, while building LESSICONS to reach and teach each future leader. And in turn, our learners will create their own life lessons while you support them, have fun with them, and encourage them to chase their wildest dreams.

YOU are an AWARD WINNING TEACHER and YOU have the gifts to inspire JOY!

#InspiringJOY

Works Cited

- Appel, H. (2020). Award Winning Culture: Building School-Wide Intentionality and Action Through Character, Excellence, and Community. Edugladiators.
- Appel, H., & Appel, J. (n.d.). AWARD WINNING CULTURE. Retrieved September 26, 2020, from http://www.awardwinningculture.com/#/
- Appel, J. (2020). Award Winning Dog. Award Winning Culture.
- Appel, J. (2020). TEACH BETTER. Posted July 25, 2020, from https://www.teachbetter.com/blog/sel-in-the-new-normal/
- ASCD: Professional Learning & Community for Educators. (n.d.). Www.Ascd.Org. http://www.ascd.org/
- Burgess, D. (2018). Teach Like a Pirate: increase student engagement, boost your creativity, and transform your life as an educator. Dave Burgess Consulting, Inc.
- Burgess, S., & Houf, B. (2017). Lead Like a Pirate: make school amazing for your students and staff. Dave Burgess Consulting, Inc.
- Cain, S. (2013). Quiet: the power of introverts in a world that can't stop talking. Penguin Books.
- Casas, J. (2017). Culturize: every student, every day, whatever it takes. Dave Burgess Consulting, Incorporated.
- CASEL - CASEL. (2019). Casel.Org. https://casel.org/
- Cook, Clayton. 2018, Cultivating Positive Teacher–Student Relationships: Preliminary Evaluation of the Establish–Maintain–Restore (EMR) Method, www.researchgate.net/publication/328757668_Cultivating_Positive_Teacher-Student_Relationships_Preliminary_Evaluation_of_the_Establish-Maintain-Restore_EMR_Method.
- Cook, C. R., Fiat, A., Larson, M., Daikos, C., Slemrod, T., Holland, E. A., Thayer, A. J., & Renshaw, T. (2018). Positive Greetings at the Door: Evaluation of a Low-Cost, High-Yield Proactive Classroom Management Strategy. *Journal of Positive Behavior Interventions*, *20*(3), 149–159. https://doi.org/10.1177/1098300717753831
- Couros, G., & Novak, K. (2019). *Innovate inside the box: empowering learners through UDL and the Innovator's Mindset*. Published By Impress, A Division Of Dave Burgess Consulting, Inc.
- David, Susan. *Emotional Agility: Get Unstuck, Embrace Change, and Thrive in Work and Life.* Penguin USA, 2018.
- Doidge, Norman. *The Brain That Changes Itself: Stories of Personal Triumph from the Frontiers of Brain Science.* ReadHowYouWant, 2017.
- Dornfeld, Kayla. *Top Dog Teaching*, 1 Jan. 1970, www.topdogteaching.com/.
- *Endometriosis Foundation of America.* (2020, May 28). Endometriosis: Causes - Symptoms - Diagnosis - and Treatment. https://www.endofound.org/

WORKS CITED

- Felicello, K., & Armida, G. (2019). The Teacher and The Admin: Making Schools Better for Kids. Edugladiators.
- Frayer, D. (2001). Frayer Model.
- Geurin, D. (2017). Future Driven: Will Your Students Thrive In An Unpredictable World? David Geurin.
- Hall, P. (2020, February 12). What is a culture of safety? [Blog post]. Fostering Resilient Learners.
- Hammond, Z. (2015). Culturally Responsive Teaching & The Brain. Corwin.
- Hunter, J. C. (2012). The Servant: a simple story about the true essence of leadership. Crown Business.
- Jagers, Robert. 2019 SEL Exchange: Building a Culture of Equity Through SEL. YouTube, 2019, youtu.be/6VRRjGSBJh0.
- Judith Warren Little, & Milbrey Wallin Mclaughlin. (1993). Teachers' work: individuals, colleagues, and contexts. Teachers College Press.
- Larson, J. (Director). (1994). Rent. New York Theatre Workshop.
- Love, Bettina. "How Schools Are 'Spirit Murdering' Black and Brown Students." Education Week, 2019.
- Love, Bettina. 6 Ways to be an Antiracist Educator. YouTube, 2020, https://youtu.be/UM3Lfk751cg.
- Love, B.. Bettina Love. Retrieved October 30, 2020, from https://bettinalove.com/
- Morin, Amy. 13 Things Mentally Strong People Don't Do: Take Back Your Power, Embrace Change, Face Your Fears, and Train Your Brain for Happiness and Success. Harpercollins Publishers, 2015.
- Nan, K., & Maslyk, J. (2019). All In: Taking a Gamble in Education. EduMatch.
- Norlin, J., & Kraft, H. (n.d.). CharacterStrong. Retrieved September 26, 2020, from https://www.characterstrong.com/
- Obama, M. (2020). Michelle Obama Podcast. Spotify.
- PBIS Rewards. (2018). PBIS Rewards. https://www.pbisrewards.com/
- Pearlman, B. (2020). Maslow Before Bloom. Bryan Pearlman.
- Pink, D. H. (2018). DRIVE: the surprising truth about what motivates us. Canongate Books Ltd.
- Siegel, D., & Bryson, T. P. (2012). The whole-brain child: 12 revolutionary strategies to nurture your child's developing mind. New York: Random House.
- Simmons, Dena. Dena N. Simmons, Ed.D. 2020, https://www.denasimmons.com/
- Strobel, J., & Barneveld, A. V. (n.d.). When is PBL More Effective? A Meta-synthesis of Meta-analyses Comparing PBL to Conventional Classrooms. Retrieved from https://docs.lib.purdue.edu/ijpbl/vol3/iss1/4/
- Teach Better. (2017). Teach Better. https://www.teachbetter.com/
- Van Marter Souers, K., & Hall, P. (2019). Relationship, Responsibility, and Regulation: Trauma-Invested Practices for Fostering Resilient Learners. ASCD.

- Vega, V. (2015, December 01). Project-Based Learning Research Review. Retrieved from https://www.edutopia.org/pbl-research-learning-outcomes#:~:text=Studies comparing learning outcomes for,tests, improves problem-solving and
- Video Conferencing, Web Conferencing, Webinars, Screen Sharing. (2018). Zoom Video. https://zoom.us/
- Walker, A., & Leary, H. (n.d.). A Problem Based Learning Meta Analysis: Differences Across Problem Types, Implementation Types, Disciplines, and Assessment Levels. Retrieved from https://docs.lib.purdue.edu/ijpbl/vol3/iss1/3/
- Yale. Yale Center for Emotional Intelligence. 2020, https://www.ycei.org/ruler

Acknowledgements

As a child I dreamed of writing a book someday, but never thought I would actually accomplish this goal. I couldn't have done this without the help of so many people.

First of all thank you to my husband Hans, you have been my biggest cheerleader and advocate! Thank you for always believing in me and putting up with all of my crazy ideas. You have grown up with me and we have been through so much together, thank you for always being there!

Thank you to Sammy, Ginger, Maya, and Winnie, my 4 legged daughters. You gave me the chance to be a mom and I am grateful for all 4 of you and the love that you have shown me. I love being your dog mom!

Thank you to my mom and dad for always supporting me. You always believed in me even when I didn't. Thank you for being the best parents a girl could ask for.

Thank you Ann for being my second mom. You inspired me to be the strong independent person that I am today! Thank you for teaching me that girls can do anything they put their minds to!

Thank you to my big brother Jason, and my 3 cousins, Brian, Scott and Conor. You helped to make me the tough person I am today. Always letting me be one of the boys and play outside with you.

Thank you to Malaika for being the best college roommate anyone could have asked for. You are always so encouraging and I am so grateful for our friendship!

Thank you to all the rest of my family and friends--you have inspired me in so many ways!

Thank you Julie Woodard for the amazing sketchnotes for each unit!

Thank you to my Teach Better Family. You are a great support system for so many educators around the country and I am grateful to be part of your awesomeness.

Thank you to all my amazing teachers, I wanted to grow up and be a teacher just like you. Special shoutout to Mrs. Belgard, Mrs. Blair, Mr. Chubb, Mr. Sevigny, Mr. Landers, and Dr. Jurenka.

Inspiring Joy

Thank you to my Wildcat Nation family, I wouldn't be the teacher I am today without all of you! Special shoutout to Kim Hobbick, Chantelle Freeman, Ben Brost, and Ann Fraser you were the best teammates anyone could ask for!

Thank you to my PLN, I wouldn't have written this book without your inspiration!

Thank you to all the thousands of authors for writing your books. I would not be the person I am today without your books. Literature helped me make sense of the world and to understand myself as a woman and a teacher!

But most of all...THANK YOU to all of my students (past, present, and future) for inspiring me to be the best teacher possible...EVERY DAY... and for all the times you made me laugh! I am grateful to your parents who gave me the honor of having you in my class. Each one of you makes me eternally proud!

About the Author

Jennifer Appel is an educator, coach, speaker, and writer. She's the Co-host of the Award Winning Culture podcast and the Co-Creator of Award Winning Culture. In addition to being the author of: *Inspiring JOY: A Revolutionary Lesson Planning Framework for Teaching the Whole Learner*, she's the author of a line of picture books focusing on social emotional learning and character education which includes, *Award Winning Dog* and *I'm WHO*. Furthermore, Jennifer has been a contributor on two books: *Teacher's Deserve It* and *Expedition Science.*

Her passion for learning comes from growing up in an education driven family (4th generation) and wanting to inspire and serve others. She is driven to create an environment where all students are able to learn and become passionate about supporting others.

Jennifer has been a teacher and coach for 22 years at Enterprise Middle School. In 2018, EMS was awarded the ASCD Whole Child Award for the State of Washington and the Global "Class Act Award" for creating a culture of excellence through kindness, service, and empathy. Additionally, they were selected as a finalist in the 2019 PBIS Film Festival and took top prize in the Community, Parents, and Staff category.

Jennifer has written blogs and lesson design for CharacterStrong and Teach Better. She was selected for the Washington State Reading Cadre and spent 10 years teaching graduate and undergraduate classes at Heritage University.

Jennifer is a part of the coveted Teach Better Speakers Network. She presents at conferences, schools, and districts all over the country. Topics include: Inspiring JOY, Creating an Award Winning Culture, Amplifying Student Voice, Student-Led Podcasting, Infusing SEL into PBL, and Supporting PBIS Through Servant Leadership.

In 2018, Jennifer helped launch a blog about School Culture and helped roll out a student-led leadership podcast called Award Winning Culture: Hosted by Wildcat Nation, which can be subscribed, listened or reviewed on iTunes Apple Podcasts, Stitcher, Google Play, Spotify, PodBean, and Libsyn.

Jennifer can be contacted through email at awardwinningculture@gmail.com. You can follow her on twitter or instagram @jennifermappel. Follow AWC on Twitter @awculture or on instagram @awardwinningculture.

#AwardWinningCulture   #InspiringJOY

FREE DOWNLOADS, LESSON PLANS, AND MORE
AWARDWINNINGCULTURE.COM

More From Award Winning Culture

Available at awardwinningculture.com or Amazon

Award Winning Dog (Book #1)
by: Jennifer Appel

Little Maya is a sweet puppy born into an incredibly successful family. But after bouncing between several homes and multiple failed attempts to prove she belongs, Maya seeks the advice of three special friends to put her on a path to self discovery. Take a walk with Maya, as she finds the secrets to becoming award winning.

I'm WHO... (Book #2)
by: Jennifer Appel

To the outside world, Ginger is an award winning dog who seems to have the perfect life. Despite her show stopping beauty, she conquers daily internal thoughts of overwhelming stress and anxiety that challenge her emotional well-being. With the help of a wise old friend, vivid imagery, and calm surroundings, Ginger creates a powerful learning moment to take back control over her own JOY.

CPSIA information can be obtained
at www.ICGtesting.com
Printed in the USA
FSHW021439040821
83681FS